THE SCARLET LETTER

Nathaniel Hawthorne

AUTHORED by J. Nicholas Smith
UPDATED AND REVISED by Soman Chainani, August 15, 2007, and
Adam Kissel,

COVER DESIGN by Table XI Partners LLC
COVER PHOTO by Olivia Verma and © 2005 GradeSaver, LLC

BOOK DESIGN by Table XI Partners LLC

Published by GradeSaver LLC, www.gradesaver.com

First published in the United States of America by GradeSaver LLC. 1999

GRADESAVER, the GradeSaver logo and the phrase "Getting you the grade
since 1999" are registered trademarks of GradeSaver, LLC

ISBN 978-1-60259-113-4

Printed in the United States of America

For other products and additional information please visit

Table of Contents

Table of Contents

Biography of Nathaniel Hawthorne (1804-1864)

Nathaniel Hawthorne was born on July 4, 1804, in Salem, Massachusetts, a descendant of a long line of Puritan ancestors including John Hathorne, a presiding magistrate in the Salem witch trials. After his father was lost at sea when Nathaniel was only four, his mother became overly protective and pushed him toward relatively isolated pursuits. Hawthorne's childhood left him overly shy and bookish, which molded his life as a writer.

Hawthorne turned to writing after his graduation from Bowdoin College. His first novel, Fanshawe, was unsuccessful and Hawthorne himself disavowed it as amateurish. He wrote several successful short stories, however, including "My Kinsman, Major Molyneaux," "Roger Malvin's Burial," and "Young Goodman Brown." Still, his insufficient earnings as a writer forced Hawthorne to enter a career as a Boston Custom House measurer in 1839. After three years Hawthorne was dismissed from his job with the Salem Custom House. By 1842, his writing finally gave Hawthorne a sufficient income to marry Sophia Peabody and move to The Manse in Concord, which was the center of the Transcendental movement. Hawthorne returned to Salem in 1845, where he was appointed surveyor of the Boston Custom House by President James Polk, but he was dismissed from this post when Zachary Taylor became president. Hawthorne then devoted himself to his most famous novel, The Scarlet Letter. He zealously worked on the novel with a determination he had not known before. His intense suffering infused the novel with imaginative energy, leading him to describe it as a "hell-fired story." On February 3, 1850, Hawthorne read the final pages to his wife. He wrote, "It broke her heart and sent her to bed with a grievous headache, which I look upon as a triumphant success."

The Scarlet Letter was an immediate success that allowed Hawthorne to devote himself to his writing. He left Salem for a temporary residence in Lenox, a small town in the Berkshires, where he completed the romance The House of the Seven Gables in 1851. While in Lenox, Hawthorne became acquainted with Herman Melville and became a major proponent of Melville's work, but their friendship became strained. Hawthorne's subsequent novels, The Blithedale Romance--based on his years of communal living at Brook Farm--and the romance The Marble Faun were both considered disappointments. Hawthorne supported himself through another political post, the consulship in Liverpool, which he was given for writing a campaign biography for Franklin Pierce.

In 1852, after the publication of The Blithedale Romance, Hawthorne returned to Concord and bought a house called Hillside, owned by Louisa May Alcott's family. Hawthorne renamed it The Wayside. He went on to travel and live in France and Italy for a spell, but he returned to The Wayside just before the Civil War began. Indeed, he would publish an article entitled "Chiefly About War Matters" for the

Atlantic Monthly just before he fell ill, detailing the account of his travels to the Virginia battlefields of Manassas and Harpers Ferry and to the White House.

Hawthorne passed away on May 19, 1864, in Plymouth, New Hampshire, after a long period of illness during which he suffered severe bouts of dementia. Hawthorne was buried in Sleepy Hollow Cemetery in Concord, Massachusetts. Emerson described his life with the words "painful solitude." Hawthorne had maintained a strong friendship with Franklin Pierce, but otherwise he had had few intimates and little engagement with any sort of social life.

A number of his unfinished works were published posthumously. His works remain notable for their treatment of guilt and the complexities of moral choices.

About The Scarlet Letter

Published in 1850, The Scarlet Letter is considered Nathaniel Hawthorne's most famous novel--and the first quintessentially American novel in style, theme, and language. Set in seventeenth-century Puritan Massachusetts, the novel centers around the travails of Hester Prynne, who gives birth to a daughter Pearl after an adulterous affair. Hawthorne's novel is concerned with the effects of the affair rather than the affair itself, using Hester's public shaming as a springboard to explore the lingering taboos of Puritan New England in contemporary society.

The Scarlet Letter was an immediate success for a number of reasons. First and foremost, the United States was still a relatively new society, less than one hundred years old at the time of the novel's publication. Indeed, still tied to Britain in its cultural formation, Hawthorne's novel offered a uniquely American style, language, set of characters, and--most importantly--a uniquely American central dilemma. Besides entertainment, then, Hawthorne's novel had the possibility of goading change, since it addressed a topic that was still relatively controversial, even taboo. Certainly Puritan values had eased somewhat by 1850, but not enough to make the novel completely welcome. It was to some degree a career-threatening decision to center his novel around an adulterous affair (but compare the plot of Fielding's Tom Jones).

But Hawthorne was not concerned with a prurient affair here, though the novel's characters are. Hawthorne chose to leave out the details of the adulterous rendezvous between Hester and Dimmesdale entirely. Instead, he was concerned with the aftermath of the affair--the shaming of Hester, the raising of a child borne of sin, and the values of a society that would allow a sin to continue to be punished long after it would seem reasonable. Hawthorne takes advantage of his greatest assets as a writer--the interiority of his writing, his exploration of thoughts and emotions--and uses them to humanize all the parties involved in the affair, as well as to demonize the thoughts that become consumed by it. Chillingworth, notably, becomes the embodiment of Puritan values, which led people to lynch and destroy in the name of God but motivated in large measure by the people's own repressed sins of lust, greed, and envy.

The Scarlet Letter also became intensely popular upon publication because it had the good fortune of becoming one of America's first mass-published books. Before The Scarlet Letter, books in America usually were handmade, sold one by one in small numbers. But Hawthorne's novel benefited from a machine press, and its first run of 2,500 copies sold out immediately. As a result, then, The Scarlet Letter benefited not only from its implicit controversial subject matter but also from an unusually large available readership. Readers who agreed or disagreed with the book's choices, however subtly, could spread the word. The novel became the equivalent of a seminal political tract--and the subject of endless discussion and debate, no doubt influencing social change. The novel also benefited because of Hawthorne's support and respect among New England's literary establishment (he would soon become good friends with Herman Melville). Thus, the novel became popular not only with the masses. It was heralded as "appropriate" reading despite its attention to adulterous love.

The Scarlet Letter has been adapted many times on film, on television, and on the stage. The first film was a 1917 black-and-white silent film, while the most recent--and much maligned--film version opened in 1995 starring Demi Moore and Gary Oldman.

Character List

Arthur Dimmesdale

Arthur Dimmesdale is a respected minister in Boston and the father of Pearl. While Hester waited for her husband to arrive from Amsterdam, she met Dimmesdale and had an adulterous affair with him, which led to the birth of their daughter. While Hester is publicly shamed for the adultery, Dimmesdale must suffer the ignominy quietly since no one knows of his culpability. The suffering begins to take its physical toll, especially since Hester's husband Chillingworth seeks to destroy Dimmesdale and is a constant reminder of the guilt and shame he harbors from his affair with Hester. At the very end of the novel, Dimmesdale admits to being Pearl's father and reveals that he has a scarlet letter branded into his flesh. He dies upon the scaffold while holding Hester's hand.

Black Man

a nickname for the devil. The legend speaks of a Black Man who inhabits the woods and gets people to write their names in his book, using their own blood as ink.

General Miller

the oldest inhabitant of the Customs House. He has the independent position of Collector, which allows him to avoid the politicized shuffling of positions. He also protects the other men from being fired, which is why many of the employees are old.

Governor Bellingham

the former governor, who believes Hester should not be allowed to raise Pearl since it would only lead to the child's spiritual demise. He decides to allow Pearl to stay with her mother after Dimmesdale pleads on her behalf.

Hester Prynne

Hester Prynne, the protagonist of the novel, is the mother of Pearl. She must wear the scarlet letter *A* on her body as punishment for her adulterous affair with Arthur Dimmesdale, the town minister. Hester is married to Roger Chillingworth, but while Hester awaited her husband's arrival from Amsterdam, she met Dimmesdale and engaged in the adulterous affair, which led to Pearl's birth. Hester is never quite penitent for her "crime," if only because she cannot understand how her punishments could be so harsh. When Governor Bellingham orders Pearl to be taken away from her, Hester wonders whether a woman must die for following her heart, prompting Dimmesdale to intercede as a subtle way of taking responsibility for the affair. Hester learns that Chillingworth is seeking to destroy Dimmesdale, and she decides that her marriage was never sanctified in the first place, for her husband has the seething rage of the devil himself. Hester is thus paired with

Dimmesdale upon the scaffold for his final moments.

Inspector

The Inspector is the patriarch of the Customs House. His father created the post for him, and he has retained it ever since. He is considered one of the happiest workers, likely because he knows he will never be removed from his post.

John Wilson

the eldest clergyman in Boston and a friend of Arthur Dimmesdale.

Jonathan Pue

an ancient surveyor of the Customs House. Hawthorne, as narrator, claims to have found a package with his name on it, containing the story of the novel.

Mistress Hibbins

the sister of Governor Bellingham. She is killed for being a witch after the novel's events. She routinely sneaks into the woods during the night to conduct covert business in the service of "The Black Man."

Pearl

Hester's daughter. Pearl is characterized as a living version of the scarlet letter. She constantly causes her mother and Dimmesdale torment and anguish throughout the novel with her ability to at once state the truth and deny it when it is most necessary. Pearl is described as extremely beautiful but lacking Christian decency. After Arthur Dimmesdale dies, Pearl's wildness eases, and she eventually marries.

Roger Chillingworth

Hester's husband from the Netherlands. Chillingworth arrives in Boston on the day that Hester is publicly shamed and forced to wear the scarlet letter. He vows revenge on the father of Pearl, and he soon moves in with Arthur Dimmesdale, who Chillingworth knows has committed adultery with his wife. His revenge is frustrated at the end of the novel, when Dimmesdale reveals that he is Pearl's father before dying. Chillingworth, having lost the object of his hatred, dies soon thereafter.

Major Themes

Public Guilt vs. Private Guilt

Perhaps the foremost purpose of The Scarlet Letter is to illustrate the difference between shaming someone in public and allowing him or her to suffer the consequences of an unjust act privately. According to the legal statutes at the time and the prevailing sentiment of keeping in accordance with a strict interpretation of the Bible, adultery was a capital sin that required the execution of both adulterer and adulteress--or at the very least, severe public corporal punishment. Indeed, even if the husband wanted to keep his wife alive after she committed adultery, the law insisted that she would have to die for it. It is in this environment that Hester commits adultery with Dimmesdale, but we come to see that the public shaming cannot begin to account for all the complexities of the illicit relationship--or the context of it. What Hawthorne sets out to portray, then, is how the private thoughts, the private torture and guilt and emotional destruction of the people involved in the affair, are more than enough punishment for the crime. We wonder whether the state or society has any right to impose law in private matters between citizens. Does adultery really have no impact upon the lives of others? If not, it should not be seen as a crime against the village. A more charitable reading of the Bible would come later in reflections on the New Testament interpretation of adultery law, namely, that the public need not step in to punish a crime when we ourselves have our own sins to be judged. Each person suffers enough already for his or her own sins.

Punishment vs. Forgiveness

One of the more compelling themes of the novel is embodied by Chillingworth, who seems the arbiter of moral judgment in the story, since Dimmesdale--the minister and the supposed purveyor of righteousness--is himself tainted as a party to the crime. Chillingworth is surprisingly forgiving of Hester's crime. We sense that he understands why she would forsake him. After all, he is deformed, he is older, he has not been nearby, while she is beautiful and passionate. Indeed, we get the feeling that Chillingworth's self-loathing allows him to forgive Hester, but this attribute also increases the relentlessness and rage with which he goes after Dimmesdale. In Dimmesdale, he sees the vigor and passion which Hester desires and which he himself does not possess. Like a leech, he's out to suck Dimmesdale of his life force, not just to punish the minister for the crime of fornicating with his wife, but also to symbolically appropriate Dimmesdale's virility. And as the novel continues, Chillingworth seems to grow stronger while Dimmesdale seems to weaken. That pattern continues until Dimmesdale dies in an act of defiance, his public demonstration of guilt, which essentially leaves Chillingworth stripped bare of his power to punish or forgive.

The Scarlet Letter

The scarlet letter is symbolic in a number of different ways, but perhaps most in the ways that the sinners choose to wear it. Hawthorne's generative image for the novel was that of a woman charged with adultery and forced to wear the letter *A* upon her clothes, but upon wearing it, decided to add fancy embroidery as if to appropriate the letter as a point of pride. Hawthorne read about this choice in an actual case in 1844, recorded it in his journal, and thus The Scarlet Letter was born as Hester Prynne's story. Hester, a knitter by trade, sees the letter as a burden laid on by society, an act of community-enforced guilt that she is forced to bear, even though it seems to make little difference for her private thoughts. Dimmesdale, however, as the town minister, wears his own scarlet *A* burned upon his flesh, since it is the community's rage he fears the most. Thus we see the difference between a woman who has made peace with the crime, publicly confesses, and endures the suffering the community imposes, and a man who imposes his own punishment because he cannot bear to reveal the crime to the community.

Sin and Judgment

Hawthorne's novel consistently calls into question the notion of sin and what is necessary for redemption. Is Hester's initial crime a sin? She married Chillingworth without quite understanding the commitment she made, and then she had to live without him while he was abroad, then fell in love with Dimmesdale--perhaps discovering the feeling for the first time. Is the sin, then, committing adultery with Dimmesdale and breaking her vow and commitment, or is the sin first marrying Chillingworth without thinking it through? And what is Chillingworth's sin? Essentially abandoning his wife for so long upon their marriage, or failing to forgive her once he knew of the crime? Is Dimmesdale's sin his adultery or his hypocritical failure to change his sermon themes after the fact? Or are all of these things sins of different degrees? For each kind of sin, we wonder if the punishment fits the crime and what must be done, if anything, to redeem the sinner in the eyes of society as well as in the eyes of the sinner himself or herself. We also should remember that what the Puritans thought of as sin was different from what went for sin in Hawthorne's time, both being different from what many Christians think of as sin today. This should not teach us moral relativism, but it should encourage us to be wary of judging others.

Civilization vs. Wilderness

Pearl embodies the theme of wilderness over against civilization. After all, she is a kind of embodiment of the scarlet letter: wild, passionate, and completely oblivious to the rules, mores, and legal statutes of the time. Pearl is innocence, in a way, an individualistic passionate innocence. So long as Dimmesdale is alive, Pearl seems to be a magnet that attracts Hester and Dimmesdale, almost demanding their reconciliation or some sort of energetic reconciliation. But as soon as Dimmesdale dies, Pearl seems to lose her vigor and becomes a normal girl, able to marry and assimilate into society. The implication is thus that Pearl truly was a child of lust or love, a product of activity outside the boundaries imposed by strict Puritan society. Once the flame of love is extinguished, she can properly assimilate.

The Town vs. the Woods

In the town, Hester usually is confronted with the legal and moral consequences of her crime. Governor Bellingham comes to take her child away, Chillingworth reminds her of her deed, and she faces Dimmesdale in the context of sinner (his reputation remains untarnished despite his role in the affair). But whenever Hester leaves the town and enters the woods, a traditional symbol of unbridled passion without boundaries, she is free to rediscover herself. The woods also traditionally emblematize darkness. In the darkness of night, Hester is free to meet Dimmesdale, to confess her misgivings, and to live apart from the torment and burdens of the guilt enforced by the community. Dimmesdale too is free at night to expose his guilt on the scaffold and reconcile with Hester.

Memories vs. the Present

Hester Prynne's offense against society occurred seven years earlier, but she remains punished for it. Hester learned to forgive herself for her adultery, but society continues to scorn her for it. (One might remember Jean Valjean's permanent identity as criminal after a single minor crime in Victor Hugo's Les Misérables.) Indeed, Hester reaches peace with her affair and in that peace comes to see the town as insufficiently forgiving in its thoughts and attitudes. Pearl is enough of a reminder of the wild choices in her past, and as Pearl grows up, Hester continues to live in the present rather than in the past. Reverend Dimmesdale, meanwhile, is haunted in the present by sins past and seems to reflect (along with Chillingworth) the town's tendency to punish long after the offense. In suppressing his own confession, Dimmesdale remains focused on coming to terms with a sinful past instead of looking squarely at the problems of the present.

Glossary of Terms

apostolic

having been sent out on a mission

arduous

hard; difficult

conspicuous

easily seen

decorous

in keeping with society's norms

decrepit

in terrible condition

dilapidated

in broken-down condition

domestic

household; local

dotage

old age, with its mental troubles

edifice

a building; the scaffolding in the novel might count as a minor edifice

emoluments

benefits

eulogium

speech of praise

gules

red

indolent

lazy

infirmity

illness

languid

weak

laudable

praiseworthy

liberality

generosity

reprimand

disciplinary warning

sable

black

sagaciously

wisely

tempestuous

stormy

torpid

dull, sluggish, numb

truculency

defiance

venerable

august

vixenly

like a dangerous woman

Short Summary

Hester is being led to the scaffold, where she is to be publicly shamed for having committed adultery. Hester is forced to wear the letter *A* on her gown at all times. She has stitched a large scarlet *A* onto her dress with gold thread, giving the letter an air of elegance. Hester carries Pearl, her daughter, with her. On the scaffold she is asked to reveal the name of Pearl's father, but she refuses. In the crowd Hester recognizes her husband from Amsterdam, Roger Chillingworth.

Chillingworth visits Hester after she is returned to the prison. He tells her that he will find out who the man was, and he will read the truth on the man's heart. Chillingworth then forces her to promise never to reveal his true identity as her cuckolded husband.

Hester moves into a cottage bordering the woods. She and Pearl live there in relative solitude. Hester earns her money by doing stitchwork for local dignitaries, but she often spends her time helping the poor and sick. Pearl grows up to be wild, even refusing to obey her mother.

Roger Chillingworth earns a reputation as a good physician. He uses his reputation to get transferred into the same home as Arthur Dimmesdale, an ailing minister. Chillingworth eventually discovers that Dimmesdale is the true father of Pearl, at which point he spends every moment trying to torment the minister. One night Dimmesdale is so overcome with shame about hiding his secret that he walks to the scaffold where Hester was publicly humiliated. He stands on the scaffold and imagines the whole town watching him with a letter emblazoned on his chest. While standing there, Hester and Pearl arrive. He asks them to stand with him, which they do. Pearl then asks him to stand with her the next day at noon.

When a meteor illuminates the three people standing on the scaffold, they see Roger Chillingworth watching them. Dimmesdale tells Hester that he is terrified of Chillingworth, who offers to take Dimmesdale home. Hester realizes that Chillingworth is slowly killing Dimmesdale and that she has to help Dimmesdale.

A few weeks later, Hester sees Chillingworth picking herbs in the woods. She tells him that she is going to reveal the fact that he is her husband to Dimmesdale. He tells her that Providence is now in charge of their fates, and she may do as she sees fit. Hester takes Pearl into the woods, where they wait for Dimmesdale to arrive. He is surprised to see them, but he confesses to Hester that he is desperate for a friend who knows his secret. She comforts him and tells him Chillingworth's true identity. He is furious but finally agrees that they should run away together. He returns to town with more energy than he has ever shown before.

Hester finds a ship that will carry all three of them, and it works out that the ship is due to sail the day after Dimmesdale gives his Election Sermon. But on the day of the sermon, Chillingworth persuades the ship's captain to take him on board as well. Hester does not know how to get out of this dilemma.

Dimmesdale gives his Election Sermon, and it receives the highest accolades of any preaching he has ever performed. He then unexpectedly walks to the scaffold and stands on it, in full view of the gathered masses. Dimmesdale calls Hester and Pearl to come to him. Chillingworth tries to stop him, but Dimmesdale laughs and tells him that he cannot win.

Hester and Pearl join Dimmesdale on the scaffold. Dimmesdale then tells the people that he is also a sinner like Hester, and that he should have assumed his rightful place by her side over seven years earlier. He then rips open his shirt to reveal a scarlet letter on his flesh. Dimmesdale falls to his knees and dies on the scaffold.

Hester and Pearl leave the town for a while, and several years later Hester returns. No one hears from Pearl again, but it is assumed that she has gotten married and has had children in Europe. Hester never removes her scarlet letter, and when she passes away she is buried in the site of King's Chapel.

Summary and Analysis of The Custom House

The Custom-House

The Custom House is largely an autobiographical sketch describing Hawthorne's life as an administrator of the Salem Custom House. It was written to enlarge the tale of The Scarlet Letter, since Hawthorne deemed the story too short to print by itself. It also serves as an excellent essay on society during Hawthorne's times, and it allows Hawthorne to add an imaginative literary device, the romantic pretense of having discovered the manuscript of The Scarlet Letter in the Custom House.

Summary

Hawthorne (as narrator) was granted the position of chief executive officer of the Custom House through the president's commission. His analysis of the place is harsh and critical. He describes his staff as a bunch of tottering old men who rarely rise out of their chairs and who spend each day sleeping or talking softly to one another. Hawthorne tells the reader that he could not bring himself to fire any of them, so after he assumed leadership, things stayed the same.

Salem is a port city that failed to mature into a major harbor. The streets and buildings are dilapidated, the townspeople are very sober and old, and grass grows between the cobblestones. The Custom House serves the small ship traffic going through the port, but it is usually a quiet place requiring only minimal work.

The connection between Salem and the Puritans is made early on. Hawthorne's family originally settled in Salem, and he is a direct descendent of several notable ancestors. He describes his ancestors as severe Puritans decked out in black robes, laying harsh judgment upon people who strayed from their faith. When discussing his ancestors, Hawthorne is both reverent and mocking, jokingly wondering how an idler such as himself could have born from such noble lineage.

Much of the story then deals with long descriptions of the various men with whom he worked in the Custom House. General Miller, the Collector, is the oldest inhabitant, a man who maintained a stellar career in the military but who has chosen to work in the Custom House for the remainder of his years. As for the Inspector, his job was created by the man's father decades earlier, and he has held the position ever since. The Inspector is the most light-hearted of the workers, constantly laughing and talking in spite of his age.

The upstairs of the Custom House was designed to accommodate a large movement of goods through the port, and it is in ill repair since it soon became extraneous. Hawthorne says that the large upstairs hall was used to store documents, and it is here that he has found an unusual package. The package contains some fabric with a faded letter *A* imprinted on the cloth, with some papers describing the entire story behind the letter. This is the story that Hawthorne claims is the basis for The Scarlet Letter.

Three years after taking his job as Surveyor, General Taylor was elected President of the United States, and Hawthorne received notice of his termination. Hawthorne remarks that he is lucky to have been let go, since it allowed him the time to write out the entire story of The Scarlet Letter. He finishes "The Custom-House" with a description of his life since leaving his job as Surveyor, and comments that "it may be ... that the great-grandchildren of the present race may sometimes think kindly of the scribbler of bygone days."

Analysis

"The Custom-House" is a stand-alone section of the novel. It resembles more a tract or a personal essay than an introduction to a piece of fiction, but it offers plenty of insights that will support the rest of The Scarlet Letter. For one thing, we gain a sense of why the narrator feels the need to tell the story. As a man of youth and vigor, he feels somewhat at odds with the Puritan nature of his society. He himself seems to feel a deep resentment for the strict fidelity to rules and values that would deem his whole personality, and his ambition to write, as frivolous or even sinful.

Though we cannot necessarily conflate the narrator of "The Custom-House" with Hawthorne himself, despite their biographical similarities, we can observe the tension that both feel in their frustrations of having to choose between their art and their livelihood: "In short, the almost torpid creatures of my own fancy twitted me with imbecility, and not without fair occasion. It was not merely during the three hours and a half which Uncle Sam claimed as his share of my daily life, that this wretched numbness held possession of me." There seems to be a conflict raging internally, preventing the author from beginning his story. It goes beyond not having time to write. Instead, the question is whether the story is worth telling in the writer's society. This reflection provides a literary answer about the significance of "The Custom-House": it adds import and weight to the story to come. The narrator is suggesting that the story goes against the social mores that preserve order among the people. Having to go his own way as a writer, but stuck in his desk job, the narrator worries about losing his muse, worrying that he has "ceased to be a writer of tolerably poor tales and essays, and had become a tolerably good Surveyor of the Customs." He has the suspicion that his intellect has been "dwindling away," so much that the story of The Scarlet Letter would no longer be possible for him to write. The act of writing the novel, then, is itself an act of resistance against the increasing solipsism of his own nature, as well as against a society that would banish the artist as decadent or unproductive in a commercialized society.

The narrator notes that upon losing his job as the Customs purveyor, his soul finally broke free, allowing him to write the story of The Scarlet Letter and fulfill his true calling. Indeed, he cannot even remember his days of being at The Custom House, despite it being not too long ago. It is as if once he finally began doing what he was meant to do, his mind erased all the time he wasted, all the resentment that he associated with "Uncle Sam," who sucked away his passion and imagination. Still, he laments that in this community, he will never be afforded the respect he thinks he deserves as a writer and will never be welcomed genially. Instead, he is a citizen of "somewhere else," figuring that his "good townspeople will not much regret" him.

Certainly a reader requires some adjustment to Hawthorne's highbrow language in this chapter. It is remarkably ornate, laden with adjectives and adverbs, and with rich vocabulary. More stifling at times, however, is the interiority of the prose. That is, Hawthorne is more concerned with feelings, thoughts, and emotions than with the unfolding of a real-time story, reflecting a romantic turn after the classical prose of the late eighteenth century. Indeed, the sin of adultery has long since been committed by the time we arrive at the first page of the narrative proper. A number of critics argue that this style presents one of the first examples of distinctly American writing, with its own history and stories and language.

Perhaps the most compelling occurrence in "The Custom-House" comes when the narrator discovers a scarlet letter on a small piece of cloth along with the set of papers that become the foundation of his novel. In an almost fantastical moment, the narrator puts the letter to his breast, prompting an explosion of heat and feeling. In this single recollection, the narrator establishes why the story must be told and why we the reader want to hear it: there is an innate power in that scarlet letter which must be unlocked, which demands to be heard. The story, the letter—neither is dead. This device has been used commonly in literature—that is, when someone discovers an ancient artifact, it retains some of its power, and the finder has the responsibility to put it to rest. In this case the narrator, despite his torpid slumber of insipid duty to job and country, has been awakened to his mission, and he accepts it, revealing to us the mystery of the letter, no matter the consequences for him and his community.

Summary and Analysis of Chapters 1-4

Chapter One: The Prison Door

Summary

A large crowd of Puritans stands outside of the prison, waiting for the door to open. The prison is described as a, "wooden jail ... already marked with weather-stains and other indications of age which gave a yet darker aspect to its beetle-browed and gloomy front." The iron on the prison is rusting and creates an overall appearance of decay.

Outside the building, next to the door, a rosebush stands in full bloom. The narrator remarks that it is possible that "this rosebush ... had sprung up under the footsteps of the sainted Ann Hutchinson, as she entered the prison door." He then plucks one of the roses and offers it to the reader as a "moral blossom" to be found later in the story.

Analysis

This opening chapter of the main narrative introduces several of the images and themes within the story to follow. These images will recur in several settings and serve as metaphors for the underlying conflict.

In the manner that Hawthorne describes it, the prison embodies the unyielding severity of puritan law: old, rusted, yet strong with an "iron-clamped oaken door." Puritan law is coated, in this account, in the rust of tradition and obsolete purpose. But despite the evolution of society, the laws have not kept up. As a result, the door remains tightly shut and iron-clamped. It seems it will take a superhuman force to somehow weaken the mores that control the society in which our story will take place.

With the reference to Ann (actually Anne) Hutchinson, the prison also serves as a metaphor for the authority of the regime, which will not tolerate deviance from a prescribed set of standards, values, and morals. Hutchinson was a religious but freewheeling woman who disagreed with Puritanical teachings, and as a result she was imprisoned in Boston and then banished. She eventually was a founder of antinomian Rhode Island. Hawthorne claims that it is possible that the beautiful rosebush growing directly at the prison door sprang from her footsteps. This implies that Puritanical authoritarianism may be so rigid that it obliterates both freedom and beauty.

The rosebush itself is an obvious symbol of passion and the wilderness, and it makes its most famous reappearance later when Pearl announces that she was made not by a father and mother, or by God, but rather was plucked from the rosebush. Roses appear several times in the course of the story, always symbolizing Hester's inability to control her passion and tame it so that she can assimilate to Puritan society. Pearl too is marked by this wildness.

Hawthorne cleverly links the rosebush to the wilderness surrounding Boston, commenting that the bush may be a remnant of the former forest which covered the area. This is important, because it is only in the forest wilderness where the Puritans' laws fail to have any force. This is where Dimmesdale can find freedom to confess in the dark, and it is where he and Hester can meet away from the eyes of those who would judge them. But the rosebush is close enough to the town center to suggest that the passionate wilderness, in the form of Hester Prynne, has been creeping into Boston.

That the rosebush is in full bloom, meanwhile, suggests that Hester is at the peak of her passion, referring to the fact that she has given birth as a result of her adulterous affair. The narrator's comment that the rose may serve as a "moral blossom" in the story is therefore a note that Hester's child will provide the moral of the story.

Chapter Two: The Market Place

Summary

The crowd in front of the jail is a mixture of men and women, all maintaining severe looks of disapproval. Several of the women begin to discuss Hester Prynne, and they soon vow that Hester would not have received such a light sentence for her crime if they had been the judges. One woman, the ugliest of the group, goes so far as to advocate death for Hester.

Hester emerges from the prison with elegance and a ladylike air to her movements. She clutches her three month old daughter, Pearl. She has sown a large scarlet *A* over her breast, using her finest skill to make the badge of shame appear to be a decoration. Several of the women are outraged when they see how she has chosen to display the letter, and they want to rip it off.

Hester is led through the crowd to the scaffold of the pillory. She ascends the stairs and stands, now fully revealed to the crowd, in her position of shame and punishment for the next few hours. Hawthorne compares her beauty and elegance while on the scaffold to an image of Madonna and Child, or Divine Maternity.

The ordeal is strenuous and difficult for Hester. She tries to make the images in front of her vanish by thinking about her past. Hester was born in England and grew up there. She later met a scholar who was slightly deformed, having a left shoulder higher than his right. Her husband, later revealed to be Roger Chillingworth, first took her to Amsterdam and then sent her to America to await his arrival.

Hester looks out over the crowd and realizes for the first time that her life condemns her to be alone. She looks at her daughter and then fingers the scarlet letter that will remain a part of her from now on. At the thought of her future, she squeezes her daughter so hard that the child cries out in pain.

Analysis

Here we are introduced to the scarlet A which has become eponymous with the novel itself. Its introduction carries a touch of humor or, at least, resistance: Hester has appropriated the supposed symbol of shame as a beautifully embroidered letter, which she wears without the slightest air of anguish or despair. Indeed, the fine stitch work around the A has reduced it to an ornament, a decorative and trivial accessory.

The community's reaction to Hester, as they watch her on the scaffold, not only gives us a sense of how unfavorably they view the crime, but also suggests that there might be a possibility for a groundswell of change. Most of the people watching Hester's punishment believe that it is far too lenient. Some say they would like to rip the letter right off her chest; others decry the failure of lawmakers to put Hester to death. Yet, there are a few who believe it is more than enough: as one bystander remarks, she feels every stitch in her chest.

This scene is the first of three scaffold scenes in the novel. In this scene Hester is forced to suffer alone, facing first her past and then her present and future. The scene at once reveals Hester's past without presenting us the details of her crime, and it ends with the revelations of the consequence of this past: "These were her realities—all else had vanished."

Chapter Three: The Recognition

Summary

On the edge of the crowd, Hester notices an Indian accompanied by a white man. She recognizes the white man as Roger Chillingworth, her husband, who sent her to America and remained in Amsterdam. Hester fearfully clutches Pearl harder, which again causes her child to cry out in pain.

Roger Chillingworth asks a bystander who Hester is and what her crime was. The man informs him of her past, telling that she was sent to Boston to await her husband, but she ended up with a child instead. Chillingworth remarks that the man who was her partner in the crime of adultery will eventually become known.

The Reverend Mr. Dimmesdale is exhorted to make Hester tell the gathered crowd who the father is. She refuses and instead tells him that she will bear both his shame and her own. Dimmesdale cries out, "She will not speak!" and places his hand over his heart. The Reverend Mr. Wilson steps forward and delivers a sermon against sin, after which Hester is allowed to return to the prison.

Analysis

Roger Chillingworth is introduced here as Hester's husband, but because the story began *in medias res* (starting in the middle of the action), we did not see whatever early affection there might have been between Hester and Roger. Now, we cannot seem to find the slightest bit of emotion connecting them. Indeed, when Chillingworth appears while Hester is on the scaffold, she seems paralyzed by fear at first. And when Chillingworth demands aloud, "Speak woman, speak and give your child a father!" we suddenly understand just how distant husband and wife now are. We are still putting the pieces of the puzzle together at this point, and we are not sure what Chillingworth's relationship to Hester reayly is—does he want her dead? Does he want the child for himself? Does he know who the adulterer is? Our first priority, as readers, is to determine whether Chillingworth is still in love with Hester. For her part, it seems plain enough that Hester has no carnal feelings remaining for her own husband.

If there is irony implicit in the fact that Chillingworth is demanding Hester to give her child a father—since he should be the father of his wife's child—it is also ironic that Dimmesdale, the actual father of Pearl, has to keep up his appearances as the town minister who is to try to make Hester confess the name of her child's father. She responds by telling him that she will bear both his and her shame, and that her child will never know her earthly father. Dimmesdale then publicly admits defeat and ceases trying to make Hester tell him the name, leaving the crowd unsettled and leaving Chillingworth with a sordid mission. Later in the novel, once we learn all the secrets that Hester is carrying, we look back at this scene with fond amusement, realizing that all of our main characters are holding back the truth with facades.

Dimmesdale places his hand over his heart in this scene. This gesture will reappear and grow in significance during the novel. In this chapter it is meant to show his distress in failing to confess his own part of the adulterous affair. At the same time, the gesture of the hand over the heart is the same one that Hester makes when she remembers the scarlet letter. Hawthorne brilliantly connects Hester's openly displayed shame with Dimmesdale's secret shame by having both characters touch the spot where the scarlet letter is displayed.

The Indian standing at the edge of the crowd introduces the division between the stark Puritanical world and the wilderness beyond. Inside the city of Boston, the laws are upheld and morals are kept intact. But in the forest the laws no longer hold, and the Indian represents the savage and wild nature of the area outside of Boston. The Indian also foreshadows the dilemma facing Hester, who must find a way to simultaneously live with her immorality and coexist with the moral utopia within Boston.

Chapter Four: The Interview

Summary

After Hester returns to her prison cell, she remains agitated by the day's events. Pearl is also upset and starts crying. The jailer therefore allows a physician to enter and try to calm them down.

Roger Chillingworth, pretending to be a physician, enters and mixes a potion for Pearl, who soon falls asleep. He also makes a drink for Hester, who is afraid that he is trying to kill her. Nevertheless, she drinks his potion and sits down on the bed.

Chillingworth tells her that he forgives her, and he accepts the blame for having married her. She says, "thou knowest that I was frank with thee. I felt no love, nor feigned any." He asks Hester who the father of Pearl is, but she refuses to tell him. Chillingworth then laughs and says, "He bears no letter of infamy wrought into his garment, as thou dost; but I shall read it on his heart."

He then makes Hester swear to never reveal that he is her husband. She becomes afraid of Chillingworth's purpose, and she asks whether he has forced her into a bond that will ruin her soul. He smiles and tells her, "Not thy soul ... No, not thine!"

Analysis

This chapter marks the second interrogation of Hester, and it foreshadows key moments of the novel. In addition, Roger Chillingworth's relationship to Hester, namely, the fact that they are married, is revealed here.

There are two moments of foreshadowing during this chapter which require further analysis. The first occurs when Chillingworth says, "Thou wilt not reveal his name? Not the less is he mine. He bears no letter of infamy wrought into his garment, as thou dost; but I shall read it on his heart." The connection between the scarlet letter and the heart was already made in previous chapters, when Hester placed her hand on the letter and Dimmesdale clutched his heart to hide his shame. Thus the reader can infer that his heart will somehow reveal Dimmesdale's secret. This does in fact occur, as a result of Chillingworth feeling Dimmesdale's heart while the reverend is sleeping.

The second moment of foreshadowing occurs in the last few sentences. Hester is afraid she has made a bond that will "prove the ruin of [her] soul." Chillingworth replies with, "Not thy soul ... No, not thine!" Obviously the reference is to Dimmesdale's soul. This prediction also appears later in the novel and seems to be coming true with the death of Dimmesdale.

It is difficult to establish what motivates Roger Chillingworth to remain and seek revenge. He is an educated man with superb skills in medicine and literature. Why then would he choose to remain in Boston and attempt to destroy Dimmesdale? There are few good explanations for Chillingworth's behavior and desire to not be known. The most likely reasons are revenge and the challenge of solving the mystery. The motive of revenge is clear enough from Hester's infidelity and the damage that revealing himself would do to his reputation and future ability to marry. He also might seek vengeance on the true father for stealing his chance at a family. In that society, it would make sense to go after the father rather than Hester, and he admits in this chapter that he married Hester even though he knew she did not love him.

Even so, Chillingworth could have left town and tried to start a new family elsewhere. But there is still the mystery. Chillingworth's behavior is too sublimely cruel for that to be the only motivation, so it seems that he is motivated both by revenge and the mystery. A third possibility is that Chillingworth is also trying to remove the father from the scene in order to make a second attempt to win Hester's heart. This idea seems unlikely, but it goes hand-in-hand with the acts of revenge Chillingworth carries out in his parasitic attack on Dimmesdale, sucking the virility out of the man. As we continue our analysis, let us revisit these options to see whether the textual evidence supports them.

Summary and Analysis of Chapters 5-8

Chapter Five: Hester at Her Needle

Summary

Hester is released from prison and finds a cottage in the woods near the outskirts of the city, where she begins to set up her new life. She does not avail herself of the opportunity to escape to a new life without shame in some other city. The narrator remarks that people often are drawn irresistibly to live near the place where a "great and marked event" has occurred. He further comments that even if that is not the reason, Hester may have been inclined to remain in Boston because her secret lover still lived there.

Hester's skill at needlework, earlier shown in the fine way that she displayed the scarlet letter, allows her to maintain a fairly stable lifestyle. Still, her reputation as an outcast and loner causes a negative aura to be cast around her. Thus young children often creep up to her house to spy on her while she worked. In spite of her excellent needlework, she is never called upon to make a bridal gown due to her reputation.

Hester spends time working on projects which bring income, and she devotes the remainder of her working time to creating garments for the poor. She lives simply with the sole exception being that she creates amazing dresses of fine fabrics for Pearl.

Hester's social life is virtually eliminated as a result of her shameful history. She is treated so poorly that often preachers will stop in the street and start to deliver a lecture as she walks by. Hester also begins to hate children, who unconsciously realize there is something different about her and thus start to follow her with "shrill cries" through the city streets.

One of the things which Hester starts to notice is that every once in a while she receives a sympathetic glance and feels like she has a companion in her sin. As the narrator puts it, "it gave her a sympathetic knowledge of the hidden sin in other hearts." This point is interesting in that many of the people now accused of hypocrisy regarding the scarlet letter include those such as "a venerable minister or magistrate," people who are viewed as models of "piety and justice" but still carry secret sins.

Analysis

Why would Hester stay in Boston rather than start her life anew somewhere else? The narrator argues that it is very difficult to leave the scene of a grave event because one feels the need to indulge in the feelings brought about by the setting. In other words, once Hester is made to stand on the scaffold, she unconsciously believes she must remain in Boston until she is somehow purged of the consequences of her action. To leave Boston out of anger or the desire to banish her past could leave her unsettled for the rest of her life.

The scarlet letter itself becomes an even weightier symbol in these chapters. Whereas at first it represented Hester's adultery and her needlework skills, it now takes on two more meanings. First, the letter begins to represent the hidden shame of the community. Preachers stop in the street and address their fiery words towards Hester, and she becomes a lightning rod for all sin, for all the latent build-up of repressed rage fomented by the strict morals and codes of the society. The more the community unloads its hatred and judgment upon Hester, the more it can use her as an example or deterrent in the name of eradicating sin.

Hester also can sense when people sympathize with her, perhaps because of their own secret sins. Thus the letter serves as a gateway into other people's secret crimes, and it acts as a focal point for the shame of the entire community. The letter thus can be interpreted as a symbol of shame shared by everyone rather than by Hester alone.

The treatment of Hester worsens after she is displayed on the scaffolding. Her friends abandon her, and she must live in an isolated cottage on the outskirts of town. Even though Hester spends time helping to make clothes for the poor, they treat her badly in spite of her good intentions. She is not just an outcast, but also so low in the opinions of others that even children feel encouraged to make fun of her, even though they have not the faintest clue what she has done wrong (probably they are too young to understand).

That Hester chooses to live near the woods, on the border between forest and the town, is a clear and potent metaphor for her place in limbo between the spheres of the moral and immoral. Indeed, Hester seems to be trying to live in both worlds simultaneously, which results in her further degradation and the increasingly clear fact that she will have to make a choice. Either she must assimilate to Puritan tradition and follow their laws to the letter, or she can roam free and follow her passions and instincts while losing her connection to society. Her society barely tolerates someone living in the moral world while having an immoral action in one's past.

Chapter Six: Pearl

Summary

Hester chose the name "Pearl" to represent something of great value, namely, the cost of her virtue and place in society (see Matthew 13:46, where the pearl costs everything a person has, but it is worth the great price). Hester is afraid that nothing good can come from her sin, however, and thus she fears that Pearl will in some way be retribution for her sinful passion.

Hester spends hours clothing Pearl in the richest garments she can find, even though it seems that Pearl would appear just as beautiful in any garment. Hester's passion exists in the child's demeanor in the form of "flightiness of temper ... and even some of the very cloud-shapes of gloom and despondency that had brooded in her heart."

Pearl turns out to be unmanageable as a child, forcing Hester to let her do what she wants. Pearl has a particular mood where nothing Hester does can persuade the child to change her stance, so eventually Hester is "ultimately compelled to stand aside, and permit the child to be swayed by her own impulses."

Pearl is compared to a witch in both the way she interacts with other children and the way she plays. Having been scorned by the other Puritan families all her young life, Pearl is positively wrathful when other children approach her, going so far as to throw stones and scream at them. With toys, Pearl always plays games in which she destroys everything.

The first thing Pearl saw in her infancy was the scarlet letter. As a baby she even reached up and touched the letter, causing her mother intense agony at the shame it generated in her. Pearl later played a game where she threw flowers at her mother and jumped around in glee every time she hit the scarlet letter.

At one point Hester asks Pearl, "Child, what art thou?" to which Pearl replies that she is Hester's little Pearl. Pearl eventually asks who sent her to Hester, to which Hester replies that the Heavenly Father sent her. Pearl responds with, "He did not send me ... I have no Heavenly Father!" Pearl then presses Hester to tell her who her father is, saying, "Tell me! Tell me! It is thou who must tell me!" Hester is unable to answer her question and remains silent, thinking about the fact that some Puritans think Pearl is the child of a demon.

Analysis

Pearl is the living embodiment of her mother's sin. She is a child of passion, wild and unfettered, and as a result she becomes mesmerized by the scarlet letter that her mother must wear. Even before she can speak, she is grasping for it, as if she knows that this holds the secret of her birth, and that its power led to her own creation. Hester does not have the ability to tame her daughter; she simply gives in to the child's inner nature. What is suggested, then, is that as long as Hester herself remains unsure about the moral consequences of her affair, so long as she lives in limbo between passion and duty, we could say, she will never be able to control Pearl. But once she makes peace with her sin, Pearl may truly become her child, a child of love.

In the meantime, however, Pearl seems very much an embodiment of unfettered id. She has no interest in playing with other children and can be violent towards them. She is not protective of her mother either. Psychoanalysts might identify Pearl as a manifestation of rage, an expression of the repressed love and passion that are silenced by puritanical society. After all, if Dimmesdale and Hester still love each other, their love is quelled and silenced by law, while Hester's loveless marriage with Chillingworth is endorsed.

Chapter Seven: The Governor's Hall

Summary

Hester takes Pearl with her to the Governor's Hall in order to deliver some gloves she has sown. Hester's main reason for going is to plead with Governor Bellingham to let her keep Pearl, whom the Governor thinks would be better raised in a more Christian household.

Hester has decorated Pearl in a "crimson velvet tunic" embroidered with gold thread. The narrator comments that "the child's whole appearance ... was the scarlet letter in another form; the scarlet letter endowed with life!" When the children in the town try to throw mud at her, Pearl chases them away and appears to resemble "the scarlet fever" in her wrath.

Hester arrives at the Governor's mansion and enters. The mansion contains pictures of the Bellingham ancestors and a new suit of armor for the Governor himself. Pearl plays games by looking into the armor and then goes to look at the garden, from which she demands a red rose. When the Governor approaches, Pearl excitedly falls silent.

Analysis

This narrator does not go in for subtlety; he tends to state his themes quite plainly. In this chapter, particularly, we see the direct link between Pearl and the scarlet letter: "The child's whole appearance ... was the scarlet letter in another form; the scarlet letter endowed with life." Pearl, after all, is consistently referred to as a little "witch" or "elf-child" or "devil-child" because in all appearances, she was born without a father. As long as Hester refuses to name her father, Pearl will remain a child not only of sin but literally of black magic. Notice, then, how Pearl is the one to renew the urgency of naming her father, even more than Chillingworth. Pearl has the most at stake to ensure that her father's identity is revealed.

Inside the mansion, Pearl looks around and sees the shiny metal of the Governor's suit of armor. She then calls her mother's attention to the fact that the scarlet letter is grotesquely magnified by the convex shape of the armor, causing it to appear gigantic. It is a simple foretelling of the fact that in this house of law, this simple embroidered letter will be seen as the ultimate message of sin, perhaps so distorted in its significance that Pearl may lose her mother here after having lost her father. After all, Puritan laws have stripped her of her father, and now Bellingham will try to seize her from Hester as well.

After Hester convinces Pearl to look at the garden, Pearl immediately demands a red rose. This scene hearkens directly back to the first chapter, where Pearl and the rose blossoms become connected for the first time. The rose blossom serves as a "moral blossom" within the story. Pearl demands it as though she sees a link between morality and passion, and she may be the only one to believe in a possibility of reconciling both.

Chapter Eight: The Elf-Child and the Minister

Summary

Governor Bellingham, accompanied by the Reverend John Wilson, Arthur Dimmesdale, and Roger Chillingworth, enters the hall of his mansion. He first sees Pearl, dressed lavishly in her scarlet outfit, standing in front of him. Pearl introduces herself and tells them her name, at which point Wilson states, "Ruby, rather ... or Red Rose, at the very least, judging from thy hue."

The men then see Hester Prynne in the background. Governor Bellingham tells her that he thinks it would be better for the child if Pearl were removed from her mother's care. Hester responds that she can teach the child what she has learned from the scarlet letter, at which point Bellingham sternly indicates that the letter is precisely the reason they want to remove Pearl from her care.

As a test of Pearl's education, Wilson is asked to examine Pearl. He asks her who her maker is, to which Pearl replies that she was plucked off the rose bush that grows by the prison door. The Governor is so shocked by her reply that he is immediately prepared to take Pearl away from Hester.

Hester grabs Pearl and screams that she will die before the men are allowed to take away her daughter. Finally, in desperation, she turns to Arthur Dimmesdale and pleads with him to speak on her behalf. He comes forward with his hand over his heart and argues that God has obviously given Pearl to Hester for some divine reason, and that it would meddle with the ways of the Lord to take Pearl away from her. He then indicates that Pearl is punishment for Hester as well, evidenced by the "garb of the poor child, so forcibly reminding us of that red symbol which sears [Hester's] bosom."

Bellingham agrees with Dimmesdale's arguments and decides to let matters stand as they currently are. Pearl then goes to Dimmesdale and presses her cheek against his hand, showing a tenderness which is unusual for her demeanor. Hester takes her and leaves.

As Hester is walking home, the sister of Governor Bellingham, Mistress Hibbins, opens her window and calls out. Mistress Hibbins is apparently a witch who steals into the forest late at night to play with the Black Man. She asks Hester to accompany her, but Hester replies that she has to get Pearl home. She then adds that had they taken Pearl away from her, she would have been willing to go into the woods that night. Hibbins says, "We shall have thee there anon!"

Analysis

Much of this chapter is dedicated to drawing stronger parallels between Pearl, the scarlet letter, and the red rose. Thus Pearl is called a "Red Rose" by Wilson when he first sees her. Even stronger is Pearl's response to Wilson's question concerning who made her, when she says that she was plucked off of the rose bush outside the prison door. For all its seeming flippancy and impertinence, Pearl's answer is remarkably astute, for if the bush represents the wildness of passion, then she was indeed plucked off of it as a result of her mother's affair with Dimmesdale. The question remains, however, how this rose can be the "moral blossom" that Hawthorne promises early in the novel.

Hester's appeal to Arthur Dimmesdale marks a turning point in the novel. It is probably the first time she has relied on her relationship with the minister for support, and it makes the other men aware that Dimmesdale knows Hester better than they thought. Dimmesdale steps forward with his hand over his heart, again hiding the scarlet letter which he feels upon his breast. This also is related to Chillingworth's comment that he will recognize Pearl's true father by "reading" his heart. Dimmesdale then correctly associates Pearl with the scarlet letter upon her mother's bosom, and he manages to keep the mother and daughter together. Pearl's response is unique at this juncture, taking the minister's hand and placing her cheek against it. This simple gesture is full of meaning, because it implies that Pearl recognizes Dimmesdale as being connected to her. Dimmesdale responds by kissing her on the forehead, in a sense claiming her as his own child.

The scene in which Mistress Hibbins invites Hester into the woods to meet the Black Man largely acts to foreshadow events, emphasizing that the forest is an ungovernable, amoral wilderness. Thus, when Hester meets with Dimmesdale later in the story, and when both seek redemption, they return to the woods in the hope of finding truth outside the stringency of Puritan codes.

Summary and Analysis of Chapters 9-12

Chapter Nine: The Leech

Summary

Roger Chillingworth, Hester's real husband, is described in more detail. After arriving at Boston and finding his wife in utter disgrace upon the pillory, he chooses to stay and live in the city. His uncommon intelligence and skill as a physician soon make him quite popular. Dimmesdale's poor health and Chillingworth's interest in the young man combine to make many of the church officials try to get them to live together. Dimmesdale declines at first, saying, "I need no medicine."

Dimmesdale finally gets into the permanent habit of placing his hand over his heart in pain, and he agrees to meet with Chillingworth. The meeting immediately leads to the two men moving in together. The narrator comments that "A man burdened with a secret should especially avoid the intimacy of his physician."

The townspeople are for the most part thrilled with the way the relationship between the two men is working out. However, a few townspeople have more innate intuition and are skeptical of the physician's true motives. They sense that Chillingworth has undergone a profound change since arriving in Boston, going from a genial old man to an ugly and evil person. Thus, "it grew to be a widely diffused opinion that the Reverend Arthur Dimmesdale ... was haunted either by Satan himself, or Satan's emissary, in the guise of old Roger Chillingworth."

Analysis

The use of the term "leech" to describe Chillingworth is at once appropriate and ironic. After all, he is a physician, and leeches at the time were used in order to facilitate bloodletting. At the same time, however, Hawthorne is obviously suggesting the parasitic relationship between Chillingworth and Dimmesdale. We return to our earlier postulation that Chillingworth goes after Dimmesdale not because he is a stock character or out of any sense of moral purpose, but rather in an effort to absorb the reverend's virility, to steal his life force and appropriate it as his own, both in vengeance and for his own sake. Chillingworth realizes that he is old, deformed, and unworthy of Hester, even though he is her husband. Yet, he seems to retain the unconscious desire that if he can somehow capture Dimmesdale's spirit, he will be able to gain Hester's love and allegiance.

It is odd that some of the townspeople can sense that Chillingworth may be on the side of the devil. As a matter of morals, we would expect them to side with the cuckolded husband, if they knew his true identity. But for all their strict laws and overreaction to sin, these Puritans can sense the energy of injustice that is growing in Chillingworth's psyche; they are attuned to it. Thus society is split in half over the man, some seeing him as a helper of Dimmesdale, others seeing him rightfully as the spawn of "The Black Man," having dangerous motives.

Chapter Ten: The Leech and His Patient

Summary

Chillingworth realizes that Dimmesdale is hiding some dark secret. He therefore expends a great deal of time and energy to make Dimmesdale reveal what is troubling him. Dimmesdale fails to realize that Chillingworth is in fact his enemy. He is so terrified of everyone in the town finding out his secret that he is blind to any enemy within his own home.

Chillingworth engages the minister in a conversation about why men keep secrets in their hearts rather than revealing them immediately. Dimmesdale clutches his breast and struggles to avoid directly answering the questions Chillingworth poses. The two men are interrupted by Pearl and Hester walking through the cemetery outside. Pearl is jumping from gravestone to gravestone, and she finally starts dancing upon a large, flat stone. When Hester tries to make her stop, she takes several burrs and arranges them on the scarlet letter, to which they stick.

Chillingworth observes that Pearl has no "discoverable principle of being" since she disregards all human ordinances and opinions. Dimmesdale then remarks that Pearl embodies "the freedom of a broken law." When Pearl sees the two men, she hurls one of her burrs at Dimmesdale, who recoils in fear. Pearl then shouts to her mother that they should leave, or the "Black Man" who has already gotten hold of Dimmesdale will catch them.

Chillingworth then tells Dimmesdale that as his physician he cannot cure him—his ailment sees to come from his spiritual side. Chillingworth demands to be told what sort of secret Dimmesdale is hiding. The minister, upset by this, passionately cries out, "No!—not to thee!—not to an earthly physician!" and leaves the room.

Soon after, Dimmesdale falls asleep while reading. Chillingworth takes the opportunity to place his hand over Dimmesdale's heart and then leaves before the minister can awaken. He is incredibly full of joy and wonderment after having felt Dimmesdale's heart. The narrator tells us that he acted "how Satan comports himself when a precious human soul is lost to heaven and won into his kingdom."

Analysis

Chillingworth seems to cross the line in this chapter from having human motives to suffering inhuman possession. Indeed, although the narrator proceeded no further than calling Chillingworth "evil" in motives and in deed, now Chillingworth's soul is attacked, and he is even compared to Satan, a thief of men's souls. Pearl perhaps senses this evil more than anyone, calling Chillingworth "the Black Man" and telling her mother that he already has captured Dimmesdale's soul.

The end of the chapter brings to light some of what previous foreshadowing promised. Earlier, Chillingworth told Hester that he would be able to know her partner by reading his heart. In the final scene, he is in fact able to read Dimmesdale's heart and know the secret Dimmesdale is hiding. Hawthorne, however, indicates that Chillingworth is surprised by what he discovers, implying that Chillingworth never fully suspected Dimmesdale of being Pearl's father.

Pearl herself seems to grow angrier and wilder the longer that everyone keeps the secret of her father's identity. She dances on graves, shuns all law, even attacks Dimmesdale now, all in a raging storm. She, in a sense, is our beacon in this story, a kind of lightning rod for everyone's repressed feelings. She impels action from under the surface, much as unconscious desires demand conscious action. It will not be until her desires are satiated, namely through confession and reconciliation among the adults who are tangled up in the adultery and her life, that she will be able to live in peace.

Chapter Eleven: The Interior of a Heart

Summary

Chillingworth, having figured out that Mr. Dimmesdale is the true father of Pearl, goes on a subtle campaign to hurt the minister as much as possible. Revenge consumes him to the point that he can only focus on causing the other man pain. Dimmesdale never figures out that his strongest enemy is the man whom he considers his only friend and physician.

Mr. Dimmesdale is so overwhelmed with shame and remorse that he has started to become famous for his sermons. His ability as a speaker is enhanced by the fact that he feels far more sinful than many in his audience. He has even tried to tell his congregation about the sin he committed with Hester Prynne, but always in such a way that they think he is being modest. This causes Dimmesdale even more pain, for he believes that he is also lying to his people.

Dimmesdale also has become a masochist, and he uses chains and whips to beat himself in his closet. In addition he undertakes extremely long fasts, refusing to eat or drink as penance. This fasting causes him to have hallucinations in which he sees his parents, friends, and even Pearl and Hester. One night he decides that there might be a way for him to overcome his anguish, and he softly leaves his house.

Analysis

Dimmesdale complements his emotional masochism with physical masochism. He fasts, flagellates himself, and keeps waking vigils so that he deprives himself of sleep, all in the hopes of banishing sin from his heart. Indeed, he still believes that he has done wrong, even when his feelings have not abated, and we sense that he cannot take public claim for Pearl's birth not only because he is afraid of the town's reaction, but also because he believes he can somehow atone for the sin enough to allow him to stay silent.

That said, Dimmesdale tries several times to confess to his congregation, but each time he even suggests his own fallibility, his followers fail to grasp the significance of his confession. Dimmesdale will come to open confession, it seems, only of his own accord. It will not be found out or dragged out of him, no matter how much Chillingworth or the spawn of "The Black Man" try to suck out his soul. Dimmesdale will have to wear his own scarlet letter and reveal it to his masses, taking responsibility for his sin and its consequences.

Chapter Twelve: The Minister's Vigil

Summary

Dimmesdale, having left his house, walks until he reaches the scaffold where Hester Prynne suffered her public humiliation several years ago. He climbs the stairs and imagines that he has a scarlet letter on his chest that all the world can see. While in this state of mind, Dimmesdale screams aloud, and he is immediately terrified that the whole town has heard him. Instead, only Governor Bellingham briefly appears on his balcony before retiring to bed.

The Reverend Mr. Wilson approaches the scaffold holding a lantern, but only because he is returning from a late-night vigil. He fails to see Dimmesdale, who is standing on the scaffold. Dimmesdale waits a while longer and then bursts out laughing. Much to his surprise, the voice of Pearl answers him.

Hester and Pearl are at the scaffold because they have been at Governor Winthrop's deathbed taking measurements for a robe. Dimmesdale invites them to join him on the stand, which they do. All three hold hands and Pearl asks him, "Wilt thou stand here with Mother and me, tomorrow noontide?" Dimmesdale answers, "I shall, indeed, stand with thy mother and thee one day, but not tomorrow." Pearl persists in her question, and Dimmesdale answers that, "the daylight of this world shall not see our meeting."

At that moment a meteor streaks across the sky, illuminating everything, including Dimmesdale with his hand over his heart and the scarlet letter on Hester's dress. Looking upward, Dimmesdale believes that he sees a giant *A* in the sky. When he looks down again, Pearl is pointing to Roger Chillingworth, who is watching him from across the street. Chillingworth takes Dimmesdale home.

The next day, after a sermon that the narrator describes as "the richest and most powerful," Dimmesdale is greeted by the sexton. The sexton hands him his glove, telling him that it was found on the scaffold where Satan must have left it. The man then tells Dimmesdale that last night, a large *A* was seen in the sky, which was interpreted to mean "Angel" in honor of Governor Winthrop's death.

Analysis

Dimmesdale begins to understand that he must himself embrace a figurative scarlet letter on his own breast. This realization comes with "a great horror of mind, as if the universe were gazing at a scarlet token on his naked breast, right over his heart." Hester, after all, found freedom once she stood on the scaffold and endured the humiliation that came with confessing her sin, but Dimmesdale is still held up as the paragon of virtue in this most stringent of societies. He simply cannot bear the weight of such guilt.

As a result, Dimmesdale ventures to the scaffold at night, perhaps unconsciously seeking absolution. Perhaps he believes that if he stands in the same place Hester did, he can find some degree of peace without having to publicly confess. But it is not enough. Dimmesdale already knows of his own guilt and susceptibility to sin. What he cannot make peace with is the guilt of having preached all these years to a congregation he has betrayed with his own behavior. Whereas Hester wears a scarlet letter on her clothes and has not taken it to heart, Dimmesdale's scarlet letter is hidden, and it is slowly becoming inextricable from his flesh.

Perhaps Pearl recognizes this, for she urges Dimmesdale to stand beside her and her mother at noontime the next day on the scaffold. Pearl senses that things have come to a head, that Dimmesdale will soon confess and that there will be a reckoning for him that will set them all free. Dimmesdale demurs, perhaps knowing that he cannot bear to make such a confession, and instead suggests that he and Hester will find freedom in the dark. It is then that the meteor streaks by, illuminating them in the whitest of light, foreshadowing Dimmesdale's revelation to the town and, more importantly, the absolution that will come with confession.

Summary and Analysis of Chapters 13-16

Chapter Thirteen: Another View of Hester

Summary

Hester's reputation has changed over the seven years since she had Pearl. Her devotion to serving the sick and needy has given her access into almost every home, and people now interpret the *A* as meaning "Able" rather than "Adultery." The narrator goes so far as to state that "the scarlet letter had the effect of the cross on a nun's bosom."

Hester's appearance has also changed over the years, but for the worse. Rather than having her youthful good looks, she now seems more like a shell of a human being. Her "rich and luxuriant" hair either has been cut off or remains hidden under a cap. But she "might at any moment become a woman again, if there were only the magic touch to effect the transfiguration."

Rather than living in passion and feeling, Hester spends most of her time devoted to thought. Indeed, "had little Pearl never come to her from the spiritual world ... she might have come down to us in history, hand in hand with Ann[e] Hutchinson, as the foundress of a religious sect."

Hester resolves to help Dimmesdale by rescuing him from Roger Chillingworth. She has grown strong enough as a woman to see that her previous pact with Chillingworth, in which she promised not to reveal who he really is, was the wrong decision. She therefore decides to meet him, and soon thereafter she finds him in the woods collecting medicinal herbs.

Analysis

Now that Hester has not only publicly confessed but also has taken responsibility for her actions, the town seems to follow her lead and begins to forgive her. Indeed, now the scarlet letter begs reevaluation, and it comes to stand for "Able." Hester's own psyche mirrors this general change in opinion. For one thing, she has suddenly become more active in her desires to protect Dimmesdale from Chillingworth. Seeing her husband leeching the life force out of the minister, she seems willing to commit adultery once more, albeit in a different form now, one that involves betraying her husband in order to save her past lover. She is willing to risk punishment again in order to save Dimmesdale's life. At the same time, Hawthorne notes that Hester has begun to lose her impulsive, passionate sensibility and turn more towards thought, logic, and reasoned action. In learning to understand and take responsibility for her feelings, it seems, she has found a maturity which escapes even the most dutiful townspeople.

Of course, it is far too late for Hester to derail Dimmesdale's imminent, tragic fate. Tragedy is often sparked by a protagonist's "tragic flaw," some problem of character that accounts for the person's demise. In this case, Dimmesdale had his opportunity for redemption and freedom, but by refusing to stand alongside Hester on the scaffold, in refusing to confess his sins of his own will, he soon will be driven to confess them on his deathbed. Hester cannot free him from Chillingworth, but she can make him see the truth before Dimmesdale is forced to reckon with his own demons before the town.

Chapter Fourteen: Hester and the Physician

Summary

Hester sends Pearl away for a moment and approaches Chillingworth. He tells her that the council thinks she may be allowed to remove the scarlet letter in due time, to which she replies that no earthly power can decide such a thing. Hester then notices the changes that have taken place in Chillingworth over the past seven years. She sees that he has gone from a soft-spoken scholar to a fierce man. He "was a striking evidence of man's faculty of transforming himself into a devil."

Hester then tells Chillingworth that she plans to reveal his true identity to Dimmesdale. He is unmoved by this, telling her that nothing he or she does can alter the way things now stand. She pleads with Chillingworth to pardon Dimmesdale for what happened so that he can let go of his revenge. Chillingworth replies, "Let the black flower blossom as it may."

Analysis

Chillingworth has tried in vain to drain Dimmesdale's soul for his own purposes, and we get the clearest indication here, as Hester looks into his eyes and sees nothing but blackness and evil. Chillingworth is completely unable to forgive or pardon, and he senses with latent rage that events are beginning to happen independently of his purposes. Chillingworth, in his way, has sold his own soul to the devil, essentially disowning it, in the hopes of appropriating Dimmesdale's vitality.

Hester sees this at once, but it is Chillingworth's final verdict that the "black flower" will continue to blossom that reveals his allegiance to evil. Chillingworth suggests that Hester's one act of adultery has spawned evil that will last forever, first through Pearl, and now in Chillingworth's relentless attempts to punish her and Dimmesdale. Hester accepts her role in the sin, but she cannot accept this perpetuity of evil. She actually will be vindicated upon Dimmesdale's confession, when the black flower will lose its power and slowly shrivel, giving way to new, unfettered life.

Chapter Fifteen: Hester and Pearl

Summary

During her mother's conversation with Roger Chillingworth, Pearl has managed to play by herself. Her last act is to make the symbol of the scarlet letter out of seaweed and put it on her chest. Her mother asks her if she knows what the letter means, but Pearl only knows it is the letter *A*.

Hester then asks Pearl if she knows why her mother wears the letter. Pearl answers that "It is for the same reason that the minister keeps his hand over his heart!" Pearl then demands that her mother tell her what the *A* stands for and why the minister keeps putting his hand over his heart. Hester lies about the letter for the first time ever, saying that she wears it for the gold thread.

Analysis

Hester's refusal to tell Pearl the true meaning of the letter is symbolic of Pearl's role in the novel. Pearl has often been compared to a living version of the scarlet letter. Thus, until she is told what the letter really means, she is unable to know herself. Her role as a living scarlet letter is to announce to the whole world who the guilty parties are, something she has unwittingly done throughout the novel.

The failure of Hester to fully reveal her secret to Pearl creates a conflict that will have to be resolved before the novel ends. Pearl's persistence in asking what the letter means shows that she is starting to complete her assigned role in the story. She started to complete this role by demanding that Dimmesdale hold her hand on the scaffold, and she will likely be the one to finally reveal Dimmesdale's secret.

Chapter Sixteen: A Forest Walk

Summary

Hester takes Pearl on a walk into the woods because she has heard that Dimmesdale will be walking along the forest path. She needs to meet him in order to warn him about who Chillingworth really is. While entering the woods, the sunlight spots start to disappear as Hester approaches them. Pearl tells her that she can still catch the sunlight since she does not yet wear a letter. She then runs and catches a beam of sunlight, which disappears as soon as Hester tries to put her hand into it.

Pearl asks her mother to tell her a story about the Black Man, who is said to haunt the forest. The Black Man is a myth about the devil, and the story says that he carries a large book and pen with which people write their names in blood. The Black Man then puts his mark on the person.

Hester, tired of Pearl asking about the scarlet letter, tells her that the letter is the mark of the Black Man, which she received after meeting the Black Man once before. Dimmesdale then starts coming down the forest path, and Pearl sees him. She asks her mother if he covers his heart because he has a mark on his chest as well. She further asks why he does not wear his mark on the outside of his clothing like her mother does.

Analysis

The image of sunlight returns once more in this chapter, as Hester tries to catch a beam of sunlight for Pearl. Earlier in the novel, Hester stated that she could never offer Pearl sunlight—she had no more for her child. But now she has come full circle, enough to want to give her child light, and even enough to want to show off her child in an approving light. Yet, she cannot catch the light; the child is still without a true father. Pearl is still not at peace. At the same time, we see that Hester, by confessing and taking responsibility for her sin, has been able to heal.

When Pearl asks why Dimmesdale does not wear his letter on the outside of his clothes and keeps reaching for his heart, again we see that she senses the truth. Pearl asks this question repeatedly throughout the story, and Hester's failure to answer tends to lead to escalating rage in her daughter. But now, we sense that Pearl actually knows why, just as Hester seems unwilling to fight any more against hiding them. As long as Dimmesdale hides the truth from Pearl, his scarlet letter will burn deeper into his skin. He has traded the love of a child for his own self-preservation. Hester, by choosing her child over the superficial acceptance of the town, has earned the right to cast off the letter, something she now disdains, for she has grown fond of it, perhaps because it afforded her not only freedom from the guilt of sin but a kind of freedom from the mores of an overly stringent society.

Summary and Analysis of Chapters 17-20

Chapter Seventeen: The Pastor and his Parishioner

Summary

Hester calls out to Dimmesdale and starts talking to him. He tells her that he feels like a cheat whenever he preaches to his congregation, and he longs for a friend who knows his secret. Hester offers to be his friend, but she tells him that he is living with an enemy.

She reveals the fact that Chillingworth is her former husband, at which Dimmesdale first appears angry but then sinks down into the ground. He tells Hester that he cannot forgive her for not telling him. Hester, after seven years of desperately wanting forgiveness, puts her arms around Dimmesdale and pleads with him to forgive her, which he finally does.

He begs her to tell him what to do now that he cannot live with Chillingworth any longer. Hester advises Dimmesdale to leave the settlement and go into the wilderness where he can live in peace. He declines the very thought, but she presses him to then take a new name and go to Europe. Dimmesdale says, "thou tellest of running a race to a man whose knees are tottering beneath him!"

Analysis

Hester reveals that Chillingworth is her husband, and it is clear that Dimmesdale has crossed the point of no return. He has withheld confession long enough to have to die for his sin, as though he has traded his own soul, his own daughter, his own love all in order to preserve a semblance of self-preservation. And in return, he has lost his self-respect and will to live. Had Dimmesdale confessed earlier, there might have been the possibility not only for redemption, but also to start anew by leaving town with Hester and his daughter. He believes the possibility still exists, but the crush of shame and guilt now deny him the option.

It is telling here that Dimmesdale, at first a portrait of unyielding stringency, ultimately forgives Hester. She, after all, has committed a terrible crime by not telling him that Chillingworth was her husband, but we sense that Dimmesdale takes responsibility for this as well. If he had had the courage to confess his sins, then he never would have fallen into the power of such evil. Finally, Dimmesdale is beginning to make amends, and he is coming to believe that he is the root of much evil, which means to him that upon his death, he will open up a path to a new life for everyone else.

Chapter Eighteen: A Flood of Sunshine

Summary

Dimmesdale allows himself to be overcome by Hester's arguments for leaving, and he resolves to go with her. He is happy once he makes the decision to go, and he feels that a burden of guilt has been lifted from his shoulders. Hester, in a moment of passion, says, "Let us not look back." She then undoes the scarlet letter and tosses it from her, watching it land only a few feet from the stream which would have carried it away.

Hester tells Dimmesdale that he must get to know Pearl so that he can love her the way she does. She calls Pearl, who is standing in a ray of sunshine. The narrator then compares Pearl to a nymph and calls her a wild spirit. He tells that the animals were not afraid of her, and even a wolf allowed her to pat its head. Pearl has decorated herself with wild flowers, both in her hair and on her clothing. When she sees the minister she approaches slowly.

Analysis

The image of the forest as the wild place where can passion can flow returns in this chapter. Thus Hawthorne writes about Hester, "She had wandered, without rule or guidance, in a moral wilderness ... as vast ... as the untamed forest." Boston, trying to keep a civilized community over against the wild, remains bordered on three sides by the forest, making the wild and its amorality a constant threat to the Puritan society. The townspeople truly believed in the evil of the woods—knowing the godless nature of the wild—and thus retained their insularity in their desire to preserve their settlement's values. But it is in the woods that people find forgiveness for their sins inside the community, as Hester and Dimmesdale discover in their nighttime meeting.

In line with this forest imagery, Hawthorne compares Hester's passion to the movement of a brook's water and its seeming sadness (a metaphor that has recurred throughout the novel). The idea of a sad brook, slowly going into the forest, indicates that Hester is lost and does not know where she will end up. In this chapter she makes the decision to follow the brook deeper into the wilderness. In the woods, she is invigorated, brought to a new sense of life, so much so that she lets her hair down and throws away the scarlet letter.

Notice the title of the chapter, and its repetition of the sunshine motif that we discussed earlier. The sun, of course, is an obvious symbol for redemption and life, but it was blocked earlier by a desire to hide the truth—namely, Dimmesdale's place as Pearl's father. In this chapter, however, Hester finally disposes of the scarlet letter, and Dimmesdale takes his place as Pearl's father, welcoming her with love. The sunshine breaks through the darkness of lies, shame and ignorance, and for a brief moment light shines on this newly reconciled, peaceful family.

Chapter Nineteen: The Child at the Brookside

Summary

Hester watches as Pearl walks up to the stream and stops on the other side, still standing in a ray of sunlight. Dimmesdale is anxious that Pearl should cross the stream, and he asks Hester to make her hurry. Pearl starts screaming and convulsing and points to Hester's chest, where the scarlet letter had been removed. Hester finally has to get up and cross the stream, reattach the letter, and put her hair back under her hat.

Hester then drags Pearl up to where Dimmesdale is sitting. Pearl again asks if the minister will always keep his hand over his heart and if he will walk into town with them. Dimmesdale gives her a kiss on the forehead, but Pearl runs away and washes the kiss off in the stream.

Analysis

Why does Pearl demand that her mother put the scarlet letter back on her breast? Pearl cannot imagine her mother without the letter; it may be a centering emblem of security. Pearl also seems to see herself as the living embodiment of the letter, and to throw it away would be to throw her away—remember that to Pearl it is not a badge of shame so much as a badge of love. At the same time, perhaps Pearl realizes that all is still not well: Dimmesdale must suffer for his failure to confess, and the letter on Hester's breast may become the only living memory of her father. Pearl also could be preserving the only memorial her mother will have of him.

Pearl, as Hawthorne pointed out, is the "moral blossom" at the center of the story. She seems to be the intermediary, in a sense, between the town's values and Hester and Dimmesdale's passion for each other. Indeed, she is at once the product of their lust and the punisher of it, for she demands that Dimmesdale take responsibility for it. Pearl is not content for her father to embrace her in the woods and return to his town as the revered minister. Instead, she wants to be held out on the scaffold as his child and wants to celebrate the letter on his chest as much as she loves the one on her mother's. She is a child of two scarlet letters, but Dimmesdale has not revealed his, and her mother comes dangerously close to disposing of hers. Pearl, as the "moral blossom," will not have it. Until her parents have brought her out of shame, she will not set them free.

Chapter Twenty: The Minister in a Maze

Summary

Dimmesdale returns to town thoroughly aware of having a new perception of life. He has much more energy than when he left only two days earlier, and everything looks different to him. Three times in a row he is approached by various people, and he struggles not to utter blasphemy. He is even tempted to teach dirty words to a group of small Puritan children.

Mistress Hibbins overhears him complain that he is haunted and tempted. She stops and asks Dimmesdale when he will be returning to the forest—so that she may join him. He tells her he is never going back, to which she replies that at midnight they will soon be together in the forest. She then departs, leaving Dimmesdale terrified of what he has done with Hester.

Dimmesdale finally returns home and enters his study. Chillingworth enters and offers to make some medicine for Dimmesdale so that he will have enough energy to write his Election Sermon. The Election Sermon is meant to be the highlight of the clergyman's career to date, and it is an extremely important speech. Dimmesdale declines the offer and instead orders some food, which he eats "with ravenous appetite." He then sits down and starts writing his sermon, continuing all through the night and even well into the morning.

Analysis

Dimmesdale's confusion and changed spirit are clearly results of his passionate bonding with Hester in the woods. Still, the evil thoughts that he keeps having are difficult to explain. It is likely that Hester has infected him with her passion to the point that he is willing to break with the Puritanical strictness and start "living" in the romantic sense. But he naturally assumes that the devil is at work instead, and asks, "Did I make a contract with him in the forest, and sign it with my blood?" This reference to the Black Man, from whom Hester has claimed to have received her letter, is a fulfillment of Pearl's questions in the earlier pages.

We do not know yet what Dimmesdale's Election Sermon consists of, but we might have some ideas. It could reflect his new learning about the importance of confession and responsibility for sin, with or without including his own confession of adultery, or he could use the sermon as a chance for personal redemption. In either case, we sense that Dimmesdale is already doomed, for he has led his congregation astray too long. We see the climax on its way. Dimmesdale, more than Hester, is set up as a martyr who must die in order to teach the town about not only the sin of hypocrisy, but also the sin of denying one's heart to preserve appearances. This is the common problem of restrictive regimes, their forced denial of true feeling in the name of a supposedly greater good. Now it is up to Dimmesdale to reveal that the good for which the Puritans strive can, in the hands of a strict regime, be distorted; a regime that aims for good might inadvertently yield the darkest evil.

Summary and Analysis of Chapters 21-24

Chapter Twenty-one: The New England Holiday

Summary

Hester and Pearl go into the town and enter the marketplace, which is teeming with people. The holiday is to celebrate the election of a new Governor, and festivities are planned for one of the few non-Sundays when everyone stops working.

A group of sailors is also in the town, planning to leave the next day. Hester and Dimmesdale have worked out a plan to escape on their ship. But Roger Chillingworth talks to the ship's captain, who then comes over to Hester. He tells her that he is adding Chillingworth to the crew for the voyage, since he can always use another physician. Hester barely reacts in her outward expression, but after the captain goes she sees Chillingworth smiling at her.

Analysis

Chillingworth prevents the lovers from absconding together, which may not be quite as good to him as if he had been able to mete his final revenge on the ship. But Chillingworth's victory serves a number of plot devices and thematic purposes. For one, it prevents Dimmesdale from getting away without public shame. If he could simply leave, he never would have to truly confront the full scope of his sin, not just the adultery, but also his hypocritical failure to take responsibility for an act he repeatedly condemned to his congregation. Chillingworth, then, is actually setting Dimmesdale free, for the reverend will finally now confess before his congregation and gain the redemption that comes with death.

In preventing Hester from leaving alone with Dimmesdale, he is preserving the status quo for just a little longer, where he remains in control. He has become the embodiment of the Devil in the sense that he is seeking to gain access to Dimmesdale's body, infect it, and ultimately take it as his own.

It is clear that Chillingworth now despises Hester, despite any early idea of returning to her in marriage. It may be more accurate, however, to call this hate a form of self-loathing. The initial mistake, marrying a woman who did not love him, is finally reaching its tentacles back around him.

Chapter Twenty-two: The Procession

Summary

A large parade of soldiers and magistrates goes through the town. Dimmesdale, towards the end of the procession, appears to have far more energy than ever before.

Pearl tells her mother that she wants to ask him to kiss her in broad daylight, at which point Hester tells Pearl to hush.

Mistress Hibbins comes up to Hester and tells her that she knows Dimmesdale and Hester met in the woods. She indicates that she knows about Dimmesdale having received the badge of sin and knows that he is hiding it. She then says that the Black Man has "a way of ordering matters so that the mark shall be disclosed in open daylight to the eyes of all the world."

Hester takes Pearl and goes to stand near the foot of the scaffold in order to listen to Dimmesdale's speech. Pearl then takes off and runs around playing. The ship's captain gets Pearl to come to him, and he gives her a message. Pearl returns to her mother and tells her that Chillingworth has told the captain that he will make sure Dimmesdale gets on board, and that Hester only has to worry about herself and Pearl.

Hester is crushed by this new information. She stands still. She is soon surrounded by many people who are trying to get a glimpse of the scarlet letter on her breast.

Analysis

It is, of course, the supposed witch who can see the truth. In this case, Mistress Hibbins claims she already knows the extent of Hester and Dimmesdale's crimes. In the forest, it seems, there is no need for confession, because people live with their actions and take responsibility for them, whereas in town, there are rules and therefore sins, with so much fear and shame attached to sin that people deny the sins in the hopes of preserving their appearances among others.

Hester's location, directly next to the scaffold, is the strongest indicator that the climactic revelations will occur in this hallowed place where sins are revealed and punished. Soon Dimmesdale will join her, but no longer as the Reverend Minister with the power to condemn and guide, but simply as a man hoping for forgiveness. Reverend Dimmesdale has a terrible time, it seems, shedding his identity as spiritual leader and moral compass of the community. But, in a defiant act, he will transfer the role of "moral blossom" to Pearl.

Chapter Twenty-three: Revelation of the Scarlet Letter

Summary

Dimmesdale finishes his sermon, and the crowd erupts in loud applause. It marks the highest point of Dimmesdale's life. Dimmesdale then loses the energy which had sustained him ever since meeting Hester in the forest. He slowly walks over to the scaffold and pillory.

When he arrives, he calls out, "Hester, come hither! Come, my little Pearl!" Pearl immediately runs over to him and hugs his knees. Roger Chillingworth grabs his arm and demands that he stop, but Dimmesdale laughs him off and says that he will now escape Chillingworth's evil influence.

Dimmesdale stands on the scaffold calling Hester, who slowly comes over to him. Chillingworth bitterly tells Dimmesdale that there is no place on earth he could have escaped to, except on the scaffold, where he would have been safe. Hester is terrified that all three of them will die after this spectacle.

The crowd is bewildered by the actions of the minister. He tells them that he should have stood with Hester seven years earlier. Dimmesdale then indicates that he has secretly worn the badge of the scarlet letter the whole time, without anyone knowing it. At that, "he tore away the ministerial band from before his breast. It was revealed!"

Dimmesdale then sinks down to his knees and asks Pearl to kiss him now. She does, and "a spell was broken ... her tears fell upon her father's cheek, they were the pledge that she would grow up amid human joy and sorrow, nor forever do battle with the world. Towards her mother, too, Pearl's errand as a messenger of anguish was all fulfilled." Dimmesdale then dies on the scaffold.

Analysis

All is revealed and redeemed in Dimmesdale's final act of confession upon the scaffold. He reveals the scarlet letter that he has imprinted in his own flesh, finally shedding light on his own sin, on his own shame that he could hardly bear. In doing so, he sets Hester and Pearl free, and he dies knowing that morality will live in the body of his young child. Chillingworth, meanwhile, is sabotaged, having lost the body on which he has preyed, and having lost a soul which he believed would never reveal its goodness. As a result, Chillingworth's potency vanishes as well, and it is no surprise that he dies soon after.

Of all the characters, Pearl probably changes most from this revelation. She has gone from a child of lust and shame to a child of passion to a child of love and morality (in the confession of imperfection), now basking in the sunlight of truth and in the unconditional love among mother, father, and child. We will learn that Pearl goes on to have a beautiful, happy life, in which she marries and keeps her mother close to her heart, without the ill effects of her torturous early life. She is now our moral compass, pointing towards truth, for it is truth, worn not as a badge of shame, but as a badge of acknowledgment of the realities of human imperfections in spite of human dignity, that will ward off the evil of the puritanical culture of shame.

Chapter Twenty-four: Conclusion

Summary

Soon after Dimmesdale dies, Roger Chillingworth also passes away. He leaves all of his estate to Pearl, who immediately becomes the wealthiest heiress in the New World. Hester and Pearl then disappear for several years. Hester returns to live the rest of her life in her cottage, and she becomes famous throughout the community for her help with the poor and sick. The narrator infers that Pearl is happily married and living overseas in Europe. Hester eventually dies and is buried in the cemetery at the site of the King's Chapel.

Analysis

The conclusion seems almost unnecessary, since the story seemed to end in the previous chapter, but romantic audiences have an interest in following the characters beyond the climactic scene. Poetic justice is occurring here: Chillingworth dies with nothing more to do, and perhaps he found redemption for his vengeance in bequeathing his property to Pearl. Indeed, he found it in his heart to claim her as his own child, perhaps in recognition that he owed a debt to the spirit of Dimmesdale and that Pearl was never a devil's child. Pearl has the successful and happy life she would have had if she had been Chillingworth's legitimate child.

As for Hester, perhaps she feels the need to repay her debt of sin by helping the poor and the sick, but more likely she has turned even more fully to living a Christian life of offering help to those who society sets low in its hierarchy. Realizing that she will not find love again after the death of Dimmesdale and in the wake of so much notoriety, she decides to turn her sunshine upon those who most need it. After all, she now has a new lease on life, with the opportunity to live outside the stringency of society; she can continue to seek peace sincerely, in and from her own heart. She dies alone, but we sense that she has lived a full life, able to ascend to heaven knowing that she has fulfilled not only her duties, but also her love, ensuring that her daughter will continue her legacy of love, truth, and honor.

Suggested Essay Questions

1. Is Hester truly penitent for her crime?

   Answer: Though Hester regrets the effect her crime has had on her child and on her position in society, she sees Chillingworth's betrayal of Dimmesdale as an even greater crime. Ultimately, Hester learns to forgive herself for her sins while Dimmesdale does not.

2. Why does Dimmesdale intervene on Pearl's behalf when Governor Bellingham orders her removed from Hester's care?

   Answer: There are two possibilities: either he fears Hester revealing his name or he truly believes that Hester deserves to care for her daughter, since he is emotionally connected to Pearl as her father and wants Hester to raise her. Ultimately, we believe that it is guilt which motivates him most, since he comes to Hester's defense only after she looks at him with imploring eyes.

3. What is the difference between how adultery is viewed now and how it was viewed by Puritan society? In other words, where does the blame lie?

   Answer: In modern society, adultery is seen as a breach of contract between two people and therefore a private matter. In Puritan society, adultery was seen as a breach of contract between two people and the community in which they lived.

4. How is the Scarlet Letter embodied by Pearl?

   Answer: Pearl, in her wild, unrepressed passion, represents the adulterous passion of her parents, as does the scarlet letter. In her society, she is completely out of place, a child of illicit passion and a constant reminder, like the scarlet letter, of that passion.

5. Why does Dimmesdale keep putting his hand over his heart?

   Answer: Pearl asks this question repeatedly of her mother, but Hester will not answer her. Over time, we understand that Dimmesdale has literally and figuratively inscribed his own scarlet letter into the flesh above his heart so that he can commune with Hester's guilt, shame, and public excommunication.

6. Do people in the community believe Hester's punishment for adultery is too light or too strict?

   Answer: For the most part, they believe it is too lenient, and some advocate branding her with a hot iron or death, the sentence associated with the crime of adultery both in the New England statutes of the time and in the Bible. As time progresses, however, they loosen slightly in their attitudes, though not as much as Hester would expect. Those who acknowledge their own sinfulness are somewhat less quick to judge Hester and can see the case for a less strict punishment by the community.

7. What are the purposes of the opening Custom-House essay?

Answer: The Custom-House introduction does more than increase the length of the novel, which Hawthorne thought was too short. It also adds a frame story and a romantic sense of truth or non-fiction to the tale. It introduces themes and imagery that will appear later in the novel. And it adds weight to the story by suggesting that the actual fabric of the scarlet letter continues to hold power.

8. Who is more racked by guilt, Hester or Dimmesdale?

Answer: Dimmesdale has sinned according to his own system of beliefs, since as the town minister he has violated the values he has preached against for decades. He takes his guilt to heart and suffers mightily. Hester, meanwhile, has come to terms with her sin over time.

9. What do Dimmesdale and Chillingworth share, other than Hester herself?

Answer: Both Dimmesdale and Chillingworth conceal their relationships to the adulterous act, leaving Hester as the only person to take public responsibility for the affair. They continue to maintain prominent roles in society. Both men are ultimately destroyed by this secrecy as they become entangled in a parasitic relationship.

10. Does Chillingworth ever forgive Hester?

Answer: Chillingworth seems forgiving of Hester at the outset, and he seems to transfer his rage onto Dimmesdale, whom he pursues relentlessly. Indeed, he seems to understand that he shouldn't have married a woman who would never love him, but Dimmesdale must be punished for allowing Hester to indulge her passion. His sinister acts toward the end of the novel are ameliorated somewhat by his choice to leave his estate to Pearl.

Adultery and Punishment

For a modern reader, Hester's punishment for adultery, being forced to wear a scarlet letter as a mark of shame upon her breast for life, may seem harsh and unusual. But the punishment is extraordinarily lenient in comparison to the Biblical and legal punishments that were available at the time. Famously, the Bible used by the Puritans states, "Thou shalt not commit adultery" (Exodus 20:14). Furthermore, Leviticus 20:10 states, "If a man commits adultery with the wife of his neighbor, both the adulterer and the adulteress shall be put to death." Jesus made adultery encompass adulteries of the heart in addition to the adulterous acts themselves: "You have heard that it was said, 'Do not commit adultery.' But I tell you that anyone who looks at a woman lustfully has already committed adultery with her in his heart" (Matthew 5:27-28).

Thus, regardless of Chillingworth's desires, Hester and Dimmesdale deserve to be killed in accordance with community vengeance. In Puritan society, adultery was not seen merely as a matter between the two parties but as a breach of contract between those individuals and the community. Even if a husband wanted his adulterous wife to be saved, she could be sentenced to die as a result of the community's obligations to its moral and legal statutes.

A 1641 Boston law provided for death as punishment (the scaffold then was used only for executions, not the pillory), and in 1644, Mary Latham and James Britton were reported in John Winthrop's journal to have been put to death for adultery. But corporal punishment, or whipping, was the usual punishment in Puritan Massachusetts for adultery, signaling that the ultimate possible punishment offered by the Bible and the law was too harsh. Hawthorne's ancestor, Major John Hathorne, was magistrate in Salem in 1688, and he ordered a woman named Hester Craford to be severely whipped in public after she gave birth to an illegitimate child.

Later, even these punishments subsided. A Plymouth law of 1694 called for the display of an *A* on the dress. Hawthorne recorded this case in his journal, and it became the subject of his story, "Endicott and the Red Cross," in which a Salem woman, required to wear the red letter *A*, added wonderful embroidery to it. The admonitions of Jesus not to judge others (Matthew 7:1) were still trumped by the society's desire to punish what seemed to be obvious transgressions against society.

Now, however, it seemed that the Puritan communities had found themselves in the difficult place of punishing adultery too leniently, because many found the embroidery of the *A* too light a sentence, but whipping and execution too harsh. The Scarlet Letter offers a way of looking at adultery that would let people suffer appropriately for their own sins without forcing the society to worry about which punishment was proper, that is, redefining it as a private matter in which the society had no compelling interest to get involved. This view was already palatable to many in Hawthorne's generation, although for many others, sexual sins of all kinds remained matters of public interest. Again, the admonition of Jesus in the case of an adulteress, "Let him who is without sin cast the first stone," had not become a guiding principle in the law pertaining to sexual acts. But Hawthorne was moving minds to agree that if adultery was a crime, it was a crime of the heart that need not be punished by society, since it had its own consequences in the guilt, shame, and suffering accompanied by personal indiscretion.

Author of ClassicNote and Sources

J. Nicholas Smith, author of ClassicNote. Completed on June 01, 1999, copyright held by GradeSaver.

Updated and revised Soman Chainani, August 15, 2007, and Adam Kissel, September 30, 2007. Copyright held by GradeSaver.

Hawthorne, Nathaniel. The Scarlet Letter. New York: Signet Classic, 1959.

Hawthorne, Nathaniel. The Scarlet Letter. New York: Barnes & Noble Classics, 2003.

Hawthorne, Nathaniel. The Scarlet Letter: Norton Critical Edition. New York: W.W. Norton, 1988.

"Scarlet Letter: Critical Reference Guide." 2007-08-11. <http://www.geocities.com/ibenglish_chs/mainpage.html>.

"Scarlet Letter: Online Criticism Collection." 2007-08-10. <http://www.ipl.org/div/litcrit/bin/litcrit.out.pl?ti=sca-4>.

Essay: The Little Human A Incarnate

by Anonymous
March 10, 2000

In The Scarlet Letter by Nathaniel Hawthorne, many of the characters suffer from the tolls of sin, but none as horribly as Hester's daughter Pearl. She alone suffers from sin that is not her own, but rather that of her mother. From the day she is conceived, Pearl is portrayed as an offspring of vice. She is brought introduced to the discerning, pitiless domain of the Puritan religion from inside a jail, a place where no light can touch the depths of her mother's sin. The austere Puritan ways punish Hester through banishment from the community and the church, simultaneously punishing Pearl in the process. This isolation leads to an unspoken detachment and animosity between her and the other Puritan children. Thus we see how Pearl is conceived through sin, and how she suffers when her mother and the community situate this deed upon her like the scarlet letter on her mother's bosom.

Hester Prynn impresses her feelings of guilt onto Pearl, whom she sees as a reminder of her sin, especially since as an infant Pearl is acutely aware of the scarlet letter A on her mother's chest. When still in her crib, Pearl reached up and grasped the letter, causing "Hester Prynne [to] clutch the fatal token so infinite was the torture inflicted by the intelligent touch of Pearl's baby-hand" (Hawthorne 66). Hester feels implicitly guilty whenever she sees Pearl, a feeling she reflects onto her innocent child. She is therefore constantly questioning Pearl's existence and purpose with questions: asking God, "what is this being which I have brought into the world!" or inquiring to Pearl, "Child, what art thou?" In this manner, Hester forces the child to become detached from society. Pearl becomes no more than a manifestation based entirely upon Hester's and Dimmesdale's original sin. She is described as "the scarlet letter in another form; the scarlet letter endowed with life!"(70). Due to Hester's guilty view of her daughter, she is unable see the gracious innocence in her child.

Hester's views toward Pearl change from merely questioning Pearl's existence to perceiving Pearl as a demon sent to make her suffer. Hawthorne remarks that at times Hester is, "feeling that her penance might best be wrought out by this unutterable pain"(67). Hester even tries to deny that this "imp" is her child, "Thou art not my child! Thou art no Pearl of mine!"(73; 67) It is small wonder that Pearl, who has been raised around sin, becomes little more than a reflection of her environment. Her own sin leads Hester to believe that Pearl is an instrument of the devil, when in reality she is merely a curious child who cherishes her free nature and wants to be loved by her mother.

Because of her own profound sin, Hester is always peering into Pearl's burnt ochre eyes to try to discover some evil inside her daughter. "Day after day, she looked fearfully into the child's ever expanding nature dreading to detect some dark and wild peculiarity, that should correspond with the guiltiness to which she owed her being" (61). Hester ultimately ends up fearing Pearl because of her inability to overcome her own guilty conscience, and thus fails to command the respect a mother needs from a child:

> "After testing both smiles and frowns and proving that neither
> mode of treatment possessed any countable influence, Hester was
> ultimately compelled to stand aside, and permit the child to be
> swayed buy her own impulses As to any other kind of discipline,
> whether addressed to her mind or heart, little Pearl might or might
> not be within its reach " (63)

Lacking any form of maternal guidance, Pearl pretty much does what she pleases; her creativity leads her to make up her own entertainment.

Pearl's lack of friends forces her to imagine the forest as her plaything. However, she is clearly upset about her banishment and resents the people in the town, whom she views as enemies. "The pine trees needed little to [become] Puritan elders [and] the ugliest of weeds their children" (65). Pearl acts to use her environment as a basis for her manifestations:

> "She never created a friend, but seemed always to be sowing,
> broadcast the dragon's teeth, whence sprung a harvest of armed
> enemies, against whom she rushed to battle. It was inexpressibly
> sad- then what depth of sorrow to a mother, who felt her own heart
> the cause! (65)

Hester feels guilty because she truly believes in her heart that it is her sin causing Pearl to become aware of harsh realities of the world. Pearl responds to this harshness by defending her mother, sticking up for Hester against the Puritan children when they start to hurl mud at her. What stands out is Pearl's love for her mother, and the way she spurns these "virtuous youths" who condemn her without even knowing the reason. Pearl is a very vivacious child whose love for her mother is deep even though she does not always show it.

By the end of the story, when Hester is finally able to release her sin, Pearl is no longer a creation of a clandestine passion but the daughter of a minister and a ravishing young woman. She is only from that moment onward able to live her life without the weight of her mother's vice. In fact, Hawthorne points out that she is viewed as normal because of the burden lifted from her soul: "they [Pearl's tears] were the pledge that she would grow up amid human joy and sorrow."

Pearl is an offspring of sin whose life revolves around the affair betwixt her mother and Reverend Dimmesdale. Due to her mother's intense guilt during her upbringing, she is not able to become more than a mirror image of her surroundings; like a chameleon, she is a part of everything around her, and the changes that occur externally affect her internally. Pearl stands out as a radiant child implicated in the

Essay: The Little Human A Incarnate

sin between her parents. It is only once the sin is publicly revealed that she is liberated by the truth.

Essay: Perception Blanketed by Passion

by William Kyunghyun
December 22, 2000

In the Scarlet Letter by Nathaniel Hawthorne, Hester and Dimmesdale are entangled in self-delusion because they are both caught up in a false interpretation of their respective sins and in an opaque vision of a better life. Hester is confused by her own interpretation of the Scarlet Letter, and Dimmesdale is caught up in Hester's inspiring words for a better life.

Hester is disillusioned by the fact that she thinks her punishment and the burdens of her punishment will evaporate along with the removal of the Scarlet Letter. She feels as if she has done her share of penance. Hester asks Dimmesdale why they should "linger upon [the sin] now when "[she] could undo it all" She believes that they should not dwell on their sin and that the sin can be obliterated by literally ripping off the Letter. Hester also believes that she can "undo it all" by removing the Letter off her chest. The situation stated here shows that her delusion gives way to the misleading on her part. After removing the Letter, Hester feels "exquisite relief," a feeling that she had not "known the weight." Hester feels as if a burden is lifted from her shoulders; this is her freedom. But more importantly, Hester neglects the fact that the Scarlet Letter burdens her conscience as well. Materially, the Letter is an article of clothing for punishment and can be removed from the body physically, but not mentally. The "other" form of penance, however, is physically intangible; it cannot be cast off her conscience. Therefore, her removal of the Scarlet Letter has compelled Hester to believe that she can live without obligation to her punishment by taking it off. And this self-delusion misleads her to not think realistically, and not fully understand that she cannot get rid of her sin or the punishment from her conscience.

Dimmesdale is revealed to be caught up in Hester's vision, reflected in his reaction to the release and purge of his sin and penance. He is thankful of Hester for aiding him in his transmutation from gloom in to one of happiness. After feeling pardoned by society according to Hester, Dimmesdale feels "a glow of strange enjoyment" that had an "exhilarating effect" on him. He feels as if he is finally free from his torment of sin. Beforehand, Dimmesdale never experiences such elation; he had only known torment and anguish. But now a "free atmosphere" envelops Dimmesdale. He thinks that he can now live free of his penance; his reaction shows his child-like desire to be free from his penance. Dimmesdale describes the nature of the current situation by saying that God is "merciful." Dimmesdale believes that God has now forgiven him and bestowed "merciful" blessings upon him. However, his evidence for joy only exists because of Hester's words of encouragement. Dimmesdale says that beforehand, he was "sick, sin-stained, and sorrow-blackened," but now he "[has] risen up all made anew." The words "sin-stained" and "made anew" show a stark contrast between the "start and finish" of his change. The ensuing joy shows that

Dimmesdale is caught up in Hester's words. He directly gives credit to Hester for the change in his manner and refers to her as "[his] better angel." The word "angel" personifies a savior or a heroine. If it were not for her words of encouragement, Dimmesdale would have thought a moment and found that society, in fact, would not forgive him. Out in the forest, he is free and innocent, but in society and his community, the knowledge of his sin would be devastating to his already tormented morale. Therefore, he is caught up in a more positive and optimistic outlook and looks towards Hester's words and vision of a better life.

In the last two paragraphs in the selected passage, Hester and Dimmesdale's belief that God and Nature were responsible for their return from a fall from grace shows that their perception is obscured by passion; the imagery of the forest and the changing surroundings further affects the couple. After removing the Letter, she feels "exquisite relief" and had not "known the weight until she felt freedom." Hester is so overcome by her passion for a better life without the Letter that she thinks her "freedom" from the Letter will solve all her troubles. Hawthorne creates a scene where Hester's hidden beauty illuminates and shines upon the gloomy forest. Hawthorne uses the phrase, "a sudden smile of heaven" to describe the oncoming rays of light. This shows that Nature has sympathized with Hester's and Dimmesdale's situation and forgiven them. The fact that the force behind this phenomenon is "heaven" boosts their morale. This shows that Goad and/or Nature is at looking out for them. Hawthorne also writes that the "Nature of the forest [is] never subjugated by human law." He is saying that society's rules and punishments have no power or jurisdiction in the forest of Mother Nature. Thus, Hester and Dimmesdale feel that Nature is sympathizing in their situation by shining light and pardoning them. This shows that Hester and Dimmesdale's perception of a better life and Nature's recommendation have compelled them to envision a blockade of the world around them, and thereby impose the rise of ambitions and aspirations for a better life.

Quiz 1

1. **Hawthorne completed The Scarlet Letter in what year?**
   A. 1820
   B. 1850
   C. 1900
   D. 1950

2. **Why did Hawthorne write the Custom-House introduction to the novel?**
   A. he thought The Scarlet Letter was too short to print by itself
   B. he wanted to describe how he "discovered" the manuscript
   C. he was interested in the economic side of adultery
   D. he wanted to write an autobiographical short story

3. **The prison door best represents which of the following?**
   A. the strength of Hester's determination to live with her crime
   B. an escape route for Hester
   C. a dirty, rusted old door separating Hester from her daughter
   D. Puritanical severity of law and the authority of the regime

4. **The rosebush outside the prison door is a symbol of all of the following except:**
   A. Puritanical punishment for moral crimes
   B. the wilderness surrounding Boston
   C. Hester's passion
   D. Ann Hutchinson's tolerance of other religions

5. **The blossoms of the rosebush are metaphors for:**
   A. Dimmesdale's love for Hester
   B. Hester's passion and her marriage to Roger Chillingworth
   C. Pearl and the crime of the story
   D. Pearl and the moral of the story

6. **Hawthorne's portrayal of the Puritanical society is one of:**
   A. support for the Puritan way of life
   B. disgust with the Puritan way of life
   C. contradictory images and hypocrisy
   D. none of the above

7. Hester has embroidered what symbol onto her dress?
A. a rose blossom
B. a scarlet letter A
C. a bird for freedom
D. a round pearl

8. What gesture does Reverend Dimmesdale make throughout the book?
A. pulls at his shirt sleeves
B. rubs his brow
C. places his hand over his heart
D. raises his eyes to heaven

9. All of the following ironies occur in the first scaffold scene except:
A. the irony that Chillingworth chides Hester from the crowd, asking her to reveal the father
B. the irony that Dimmesdale is called upon to ask Hester who the father is
C. the irony that Hester is married to Chillingworth but has had a child with another man
D. the irony that Pearl will bring Hester and Dimmesdale back together

10. Chillingworth pretends to be of what profession?
A. a doctor
B. a lawyer
C. an infantryman
D. a clergyman

11. After she is released from prison, Hester goes to live where?
A. within the city of Boston
B. with Roger Chillingworth
C. in another city in the colony of Massachusetts
D. on the outskirts of Boston

12. How does Hester earn a living?
A. by growing crops
B. by healing other people
C. by her needlework
D. by selling wood in Boston

13. **What is the first thing that Pearl sees as a baby?**
    A. Hester
    B. the scarlet letter on Hester's chest
    C. the inside of a prison cell
    D. the rosebush

14. **What does Pearl best represent throughout the novel?**
    A. the unifying force that will bring Hester and Dimmesdale together at the end
    B. a young innocent child
    C. the living embodiment of Hester's sin
    D. a form of punishment for Hester

15. **When John Wilson asks Pearl who her maker is, Pearl replies:**
    A. that Hester and Dimmesdale made her
    B. that God made her
    C. that sin made her
    D. that she was plucked off of a rose bush

16. **Mistress Hibbins, the sister of Governor Bellingham, is reputed to be:**
    A. a witch
    B. a Puritan
    C. a cruel lady
    D. a good mother

17. **Hawthorne draws strong parallels between what three images?**
    A. the prison door, the scarlet letter, Pearl
    B. Pearl, the red rose, the scarlet letter
    C. Pearl, Hester, the red rose
    D. the prison door, the red rose, Pearl

18. **To whom does Hawthorne apply the term "The Leech"?**
    A. Hester
    B. Chillingworth
    C. Dimmesdale
    D. Pearl

19. **How does Chillingworth figure out who Pearl's father really is?**
   A. Dimmesdale tells him
   B. Hester tells him one day in the woods
   C. He never finds out
   D. Chillingworth becomes Dimmesdale's doctor and guesses the secret

20. **What illuminates the first scaffold scene where Hester, Dimmesdale and Pearl are brought together?**
   A. a torch
   B. a meteor
   C. a lantern
   D. a fire

21. **The fact that this scaffold scene is illuminated can be understood as:**
   A. success for Chillingworth
   B. bad luck
   C. divine intervention
   D. Hawthorne's desire to be melodramatic

22. **Pearl's role changes towards the end of the novel. She starts to "punish" which character?**
   A. Hester
   B. Chillingworth
   C. Bellingham
   D. Dimmesdale

23. **What is Hester's response when she learns that the Puritan council might allow her to remove her scarlet letter?**
   A. she is furious
   B. she indicates that only God can remove her letter
   C. she is very happy
   D. she immediately takes the letter off and goes into town without it

24. **Hester tries to convince Dimmesdale to do what during their walks in the woods?**
   A. to get rid of Chillingworth
   B. to adopt Pearl
   C. to run away and live elsewhere
   D. to marry her

25. **What does the forest stand for?**
    A. An evil place where the Dark Man lives
    B. A dark, sinister place where lives are ruined
    C. A wild, uninhibited place where passion can flourish
    D. A bright place where flowers grow

Quiz 1 Answer Key

1. **(B)** 1850
2. **(A)** he thought The Scarlet Letter was too short to print by itself
3. **(D)** Puritanical severity of law and the authority of the regime
4. **(A)** Puritanical punishment for moral crimes
5. **(D)** Pearl and the moral of the story
6. **(C)** contradictory images and hypocrisy
7. **(B)** a scarlet letter A
8. **(C)** places his hand over his heart
9. **(D)** the irony that Pearl will bring Hester and Dimmesdale back together
10. **(A)** a doctor
11. **(D)** on the outskirts of Boston
12. **(C)** by her needlework
13. **(B)** the scarlet letter on Hester's chest
14. **(C)** the living embodiment of Hester's sin
15. **(D)** that she was plucked off of a rose bush
16. **(A)** a witch
17. **(B)** Pearl, the red rose, the scarlet letter
18. **(B)** Chillingworth
19. **(D)** Chillingworth becomes Dimmesdale's doctor and guesses the secret
20. **(B)** a meteor
21. **(C)** divine intervention
22. **(D)** Dimmesdale
23. **(B)** she indicates that only God can remove her letter
24. **(C)** to run away and live elsewhere
25. **(C)** A wild, uninhibited place where passion can flourish

Quiz 2

1. **What does Pearl do when she first sees her mother without the scarlet letter?**
   A. runs to hug her mother
   B. convulses and screams
   C. runs away
   D. is excited for her mother

2. **The moral of the story is best represented by which character?**
   A. Hester
   B. Chillingworth
   C. Dimmesdale
   D. Pearl

3. **Who destroys Dimmesdale and Hester's plans to run away from Boston?**
   A. John Williams
   B. Chillingworth
   C. Bellingham
   D. Pearl

4. **In the final scaffold scene, Dimmesdale believes that _____ is visible on his chest, over his heart.**
   A. a rose blossom
   B. nothing
   C. a scarlet letter A
   D. a bright red heart

5. **What does Pearl do right before Dimmesdale dies?**
   A. runs away from Hester
   B. runs to Roger Chillingworth
   C. takes his hand and gives it to Hester
   D. kisses Dimmesdale

6. **The term Black Man refers to _____**
   A. Chillingworth
   B. The Devil
   C. God
   D. Dimmesdale

7. **Who strongly advocates that Pearl be taken away from Hester?**
   A. Governor Bellingham
   B. Chillingworth
   C. Dimmesdale
   D. Hecuba

8. **Who does Hester allow to be "swayed by her own impulses"?**
   A. Mrs. Dimmesdale
   B. Mistress Hibbins
   C. Mrs. Chillingworth
   D. Pearl

9. **The narrator of the Custom House was a Surveyor of _____**
   A. Revenue
   B. Property
   C. Resources
   D. Propriety

10. **Some people interpret the A on Hester's chest to mean what?**
    A. accomplished
    B. asymmetrical
    C. abhorrent
    D. able

11. **Who reveals to Dimmesdale that Chillingworth is Hester's husband?**
    A. Hester
    B. Chillingworth
    C. Mistress Hibbins
    D. Bellingham

12. **What is Roger Chillingworth's occupation?**
    A. lawyer
    B. minister
    C. librarian
    D. physician

13. **Chillingworth was returning from which city when the affair between Dimmesdale and Hester occurred?**
    A. London
    B. Sao Paolo
    C. Amsterdam
    D. Paris

14. **Where were Hester and Chillingworth married?**
    A. South America
    B. Boston
    C. England
    D. Netherlands

15. **In which century is The Scarlet Letter set?**
    A. eighteenth century
    B. nineteenth century
    C. seventeenth century
    D. sixteenth century

16. **Who has Chillingsworth been living with before he appears in Boston?**
    A. Indians
    B. Pilgrims
    C. Spanish traders
    D. Englishmen

17. **Where does The Scarlet Letter take place?**
    A. San Francisco
    B. Philadelphia
    C. Boston
    D. New York

18. **Mistress Hibbins is executed as a _____**
    A. adulteress
    B. prostitute
    C. thief
    D. witch

19. **Hester is known for what?**
    A. dancing
    B. cooking
    C. knitting
    D. writing ability

20. **What does Pearl do before Dimmesdale dies to demonstrate her love for him?**
    A. hits him
    B. calls Chillingworth her real father
    C. tells the crowd he's her father
    D. kisses him

21. **What is the usual color of Hester's clothes?**
    A. yellow
    B. Scarlet and gold
    C. gray
    D. black

22. **Who punishes himself with flagellation for his crimes?**
    A. the Indian spectator
    B. Chillingworth
    C. Bellingham
    D. Dimmesdale

23. **Pearl says that Mistress Hibbins called her father the Prince of _____**
    A. dreams
    B. air
    C. fire
    D. water

24. **Pearl constantly asks her mother why _____**
    A. Chillingworth calls her "little Pearl"
    B. Bellingham wants to take her out of Hester's custody
    C. Hester knits
    D. Dimmesdale keeps his hand over his heart

25. **Hester is described as a woman of "marble coldness" because she moves from passions and feelings to what?**
    A. gossip
    B. thought
    C. nastiness
    D. self-flagellation

Quiz 2 Answer Key

1. (**B**) convulses and screams
2. (**D**) Pearl
3. (**B**) Chillingworth
4. (**C**) a scarlet letter A
5. (**D**) kisses Dimmesdale
6. (**B**) The Devil
7. (**A**) Governor Bellingham
8. (**D**) Pearl
9. (**A**) Revenue
10. (**D**) able
11. (**A**) Hester
12. (**D**) physician
13. (**C**) Amsterdam
14. (**C**) England
15. (**C**) seventeenth century
16. (**A**) Indians
17. (**C**) Boston
18. (**D**) witch
19. (**C**) knitting
20. (**D**) kisses him
21. (**D**) black
22. (**D**) Dimmesdale
23. (**B**) air
24. (**D**) Dimmesdale keeps his hand over his heart
25. (**B**) thought

Quiz 3

1. **What finally breaks the spell of pain over Dimmesdale?**
   A. a kiss from Pearl
   B. a kiss from Hester
   C. an honor from Bellingham
   D. a blow from Chillingworth

2. **When does Hester reveal the name of the man with whom she committed adultery?**
   A. in jail
   B. on her death bed
   C. upon release from jail
   D. never

3. **What does Chillingworth bequeath to Pearl?**
   A. a college scholarship
   B. property
   C. a boat
   D. money

4. **Chillingworth bequeaths property that lies both in _____**
   A. Boston and Paris
   B. England and Paris
   C. Boston and England
   D. England and New York

5. **The Black Man is said to haunt the _____**
   A. forest
   B. village
   C. heavens
   D. sea

6. **Who moves in to live with Dimmesdale to take care of him?**
   A. Hester
   B. Governor Bellingham
   C. Chillingworth
   D. Pearl

7. **Pearl is also known as ____**
    A. the Rose child
    B. the Black Child
    C. the demon child
    D. the elf-child

8. **Who checks up on Pearl after the conclusion of the novel's events?**
    A. Chillingworth
    B. Mistress Hibbins
    C. Bellingham
    D. Surveyor Pue

9. **How does the narrator discover that Pearl has a lover at the conclusion of the book?**
    A. Chillingworth foretells their meeting
    B. the arrival of letters from her paramour
    C. he has tea with Hester
    D. he attends her wedding

10. **What is definition of the word "gules"?**
    A. breaks
    B. glowing black
    C. glowing red
    D. rules

11. **Bellingham holds what position in the town?**
    A. governor
    B. president
    C. king
    D. mayor

12. **In 1640s New England, adultery was usually punishable by ____**
    A. nothing
    B. corporal punishment
    C. a scarlet A
    D. death

13. **The Bible book of Leviticus argues for what punishment when it comes to adultery?**
    A. no punishment
    B. corporal punishment
    C. public shaming
    D. death

14. **The New Testament encourages what policy towards adulterers?**
    A. leaving it a private matter
    B. imprisonment
    C. punishing it with death
    D. physically beating both adulterer and adulteress

15. **How does the town react to Chillingworth inhabiting with Dimmesdale?**
    A. they don't care
    B. they don't know about it
    C. favorably
    D. unfavorably

16. **Most of the people in Boston think that Hester's punishment of having to wear the scarlet letter is too _____**
    A. lenient
    B. fitting
    C. outdated
    D. harsh

17. **Some people believe that Hester should be punished not with an embroidered A, but with what?**
    A. a pinned A in her flesh
    B. an A tattooed in ink on her chest
    C. a branded A upon her chest
    D. an A bracelet

18. **When Dimmesdale seems physically ill, rumors abound that he is being possessed by whom?**
    A. a witch
    B. God
    C. a voodoo presence
    D. Satan

19. **Governor Bellingham remarks that he used to call little children in old King James's court what?**
    A. Lords of Satan
    B. Lords of Misdeed
    C. Lords of Misrule
    D. Lords of Air

20. **When Mr. Wilson first sees Pearl, he compares her to what?**
    A. a scarlet rag of blood
    B. a scarlet cloth
    C. a scarlet bird of plumage
    D. a scarlet sky

21. **Which name does Mr. Wilson not use for Pearl?**
    A. Red Bird
    B. Red Rose
    C. Ruby
    D. Coral

22. **Who is the oldest inhabitant of the Custom House?**
    A. Governor Bellingham
    B. General Miller
    C. John Wilson
    D. Surveyor Pue

23. **Why is the Inspector one of the happiest workers of the Custom House?**
    A. he is quitting his job
    B. he is about to fire Surveyor Pue
    C. he is about to get married
    D. he knows he cannot be fired

24. **Whose name is on the package that contains the story of the Scarlet Letter?**
    A. Roger Chillingworth
    B. Mistress Hibbins
    C. Arthur Dimmesdale
    D. Jonathan Pue

25. Governor Bellingham's sister is _____

    A. Lady Pue
    B. Lady Bellingham
    C. Mistress Hibbins
    D. Lady Prynne

Quiz 3 Answer Key

1. **(A)** a kiss from Pearl
2. **(D)** never
3. **(B)** property
4. **(C)** Boston and England
5. **(A)** forest
6. **(C)** Chillingworth
7. **(D)** the elf-child
8. **(D)** Surveyor Pue
9. **(B)** the arrival of letters from her paramour
10. **(C)** glowing red
11. **(A)** governor
12. **(D)** death
13. **(D)** death
14. **(A)** leaving it a private matter
15. **(C)** favorably
16. **(A)** lenient
17. **(C)** a branded A upon her chest
18. **(D)** Satan
19. **(C)** Lords of Misrule
20. **(C)** a scarlet bird of plumage
21. **(A)** Red Bird
22. **(B)** General Miller
23. **(D)** he knows he cannot be fired
24. **(D)** Jonathan Pue
25. **(C)** Mistress Hibbins

Quiz 4

1. **On what day does Chillingworth arrive in Boston?**
   A. on the day Hester is executed
   B. on the day Hester is publicly shamed
   C. on the day Pearl is born
   D. on the day Dimmesdale is accused

2. **How many years have Dimmesdale and Hester been suffering under the shame of adultery?**
   A. 5 years
   B. 7 years
   C. 10 years
   D. 3 years

3. **Who questions whether grass will grow on their grave?**
   A. Hester
   B. Chillingworth
   C. Dimmesdale
   D. Pearl

4. **How is Hester's needlework received by the community?**
   A. it is exported to Australia
   B. it is considered fashionable
   C. it is considered too expensive
   D. it is shunned

5. **When the narrator puts the old scarlet letter from Pue's package on his breast, he notices that it _____**
   A. sparks flames
   B. glows red
   C. gets duller
   D. burns

6. **Dimmesdale's climactic sermon is known as the _____**
   A. Thanksgiving Sermon
   B. Election Sermon
   C. Christmas Sermon
   D. April Sermon

7. **Dimmesdale is referred to as** _____
   A. Reverend Dimmesdale
   B. Minister Dimmesdale
   C. Sir Dimmesdale
   D. Sir Arthur

8. **When did Nathaniel Hawthorne's ancestors arrive in America?**
   A. 1580
   B. 1630
   C. 1750
   D. 1850

9. **Nathaniel Hawthorne was born in** _____
   A. 1780
   B. 1804
   C. 1820
   D. 1840

10. **Hawthorne lived for a time in** _____
    A. England
    B. Argentina
    C. Italy
    D. Netherlands

11. **In 1857, Hawthorne traveled to** _____
    A. England
    B. Germany
    C. Netherlands
    D. France

12. **Nathaniel Hawthorne died in** _____
    A. 1840
    B. 1850
    C. 1864
    D. 1910

13. **When do we read about the details of Hester and Dimmesdale's affair?**
    A. after Chillingworth reveals them
    B. after Pearl reads a letter from her mother to Dimmesdale
    C. at the outset of the novel
    D. never

14. **Some critics argue that Hawthorne shrouds the act of adultery in mystery, so some readers might confuse adultery for _____**
    A. incest
    B. murder
    C. thievery
    D. treachery

15. **What two words best describe Chillingworth's physical relationship to Hester?**
    A. younger and deformed
    B. older and more handsome
    C. older and deformed
    D. younger and more handsome

16. **Another reason Hawthorne included the Custom-House introduction was to:**
    A. have the novel considered as nonfiction
    B. make sure it would be added to the Custom House archives
    C. enrich the themes of the novel
    D. make it approachable for a European audience

17. **The narrator in "The Custom-House" refers to America as what?**
    A. The Statue of Liberty
    B. Uncle Sam
    C. My Beloved
    D. The United States

18. **What does the narrator find in Surveyor Pue's package?**
    A. the old embroidered letter
    B. a picture of Pearl and Hester
    C. the story of the scarlet letter and the old embroidered letter
    D. the story of the scarlet letter

19. **Pearl tells Mr. Wilson that she was what?**
    A. born of a mother and a father
    B. sent by a stork
    C. born of God
    D. plucked off a pile of rose bushes

20. **How old is Pearl when she is examined by Mr. Wilson?**
    A. 3
    B. 5
    C. 6
    D. 7

21. **Pearl issues the scandalous answer about the roses to Mr. Wilson perhaps because she _____**
    A. sleeps on a bed of roses
    B. loves the red roses that her father gave her
    C. loves the red roses that her mother gave her
    D. sees the red roses outside the window

22. **When Hester argues that she wants to keep Pearl, what is her first line of defense?**
    A. "God gave me this child!"
    B. "Love gave me this child!"
    C. "Honor gave me this child!"
    D. "Justice gave me this child!"

23. **Hester says that if she has to give Pearl up, she will _____**
    A. burn the church down
    B. kill Mr. Wilson
    C. die
    D. shoot townspeople with arrows

24. **What is Hester's response to Mistress Hibbins's offer to go into the woods wth the child?**
    A. she cannot, now that she can keep the child
    B. she wants to go and show Pearl the cultish ceremony
    C. she would rather wait until she hears Mr. Wilson's verdict about custody
    D. they have no time, being late for church

25. **Nathaniel Hawthorne labeled his novel as what on its cover page?**
   A. a comedy
   B. a romance
   C. a tragedy
   D. an adventure

Quiz 4 Answer Key

1. **(B)** on the day Hester is publicly shamed
2. **(B)** 7 years
3. **(C)** Dimmesdale
4. **(B)** it is considered fashionable
5. **(D)** burns
6. **(B)** Election Sermon
7. **(A)** Reverend Dimmesdale
8. **(B)** 1630
9. **(B)** 1804
10. **(C)** Italy
11. **(D)** France
12. **(C)** 1864
13. **(D)** never
14. **(A)** incest
15. **(C)** older and deformed
16. **(C)** enrich the themes of the novel
17. **(B)** Uncle Sam
18. **(C)** the story of the scarlet letter and the old embroidered letter
19. **(D)** plucked off a pile of rose bushes
20. **(A)** 3
21. **(D)** sees the red roses outside the window
22. **(A)** "God gave me this child!"
23. **(C)** die
24. **(A)** she cannot, now that she can keep the child
25. **(B)** a romance

ClassicNotes

GrAdeSaver™

Getting you the grade since 1999™

Other ClassicNotes from GradeSaver™

1984
Absalom, Absalom
Adam Bede
The Adventures of Augie
  March
The Adventures of
  Huckleberry Finn
The Adventures of Tom
  Sawyer
The Aeneid
Agamemnon
The Age of Innocence
Alice in Wonderland
All My Sons
All Quiet on the Western
  Front
All the King's Men
All the Pretty Horses
The Ambassadors
American Beauty
Angela's Ashes
Animal Farm
Anna Karenina
Antigone
Antony and Cleopatra
Aristotle's Ethics
Aristotle's Poetics
Aristotle's Politics
As I Lay Dying
As You Like It
Astrophil and Stella
The Awakening
Babbitt
The Bacchae
Bartleby the Scrivener
The Bean Trees

The Bell Jar
Beloved
Benito Cereno
Beowulf
Bhagavad-Gita
Billy Budd
Black Boy
Bleak House
The Bloody Chamber
Bluest Eye
The Bonfire of the
  Vanities
Brave New World
Breakfast at Tiffany's
Call of the Wild
Candide
The Canterbury Tales
Cat's Cradle
Catch-22
The Catcher in the Rye
The Caucasian Chalk
  Circle
The Cherry Orchard
The Chosen
A Christmas Carol
Chronicle of a Death
  Foretold
Civil Disobedience
Civilization and Its
  Discontents
A Clockwork Orange
The Color of Water
The Color Purple
Comedy of Errors
Communist Manifesto

A Confederacy of
  Dunces
Confessions
Connecticut Yankee in
  King Arthur's Court
The Consolation of
  Philosophy
Coriolanus
The Count of Monte
  Cristo
Crime and Punishment
The Crucible
Cry, the Beloved
  Country
The Crying of Lot 49
Cymbeline
Daisy Miller
Death in Venice
Death of a Salesman
The Death of Ivan Ilych
Democracy in America
Devil in a Blue Dress
Dharma Bums
The Diary of Anne Frank
Disgrace
Divine Comedy-I:
  Inferno
A Doll's House
Don Quixote Book I
Don Quixote Book II
Dr. Faustus
Dr. Jekyll and Mr. Hyde
Dracula
Dubliners
East of Eden
Emma

For our full list of over 250 Study Guides, Quizzes,
Sample College Application Essays, Literature Essays and E-texts, visit:

www.gradesaver.com

ClassicNotes

GradeSaver™

Getting you the grade since 1999™

Other ClassicNotes from GradeSaver™

Ender's Game
Endgame
The English Patient
Ethan Frome
The Eumenides
Everything is Illuminated
Fahrenheit 451
The Fall of the House of
    Usher
Farewell to Arms
The Federalist Papers
For Whom the Bell Tolls
The Fountainhead
Frankenstein
Franny and Zooey
Glass Menagerie
The God of Small Things
The Good Earth
The Grapes of Wrath
Great Expectations
The Great Gatsby
The Guest
Gulliver's Travels
Hamlet
The Handmaid's Tale
Hard Times
Heart of Darkness
Hedda Gabler
Henry IV (Pirandello)
Henry IV Part 1
Henry IV Part 2
Henry V
Herzog
The Hobbit
Homo Faber
House of Mirth

House of the Seven
    Gables
The House of the Spirits
House on Mango Street
Howards End
A Hunger Artist
I Know Why the Caged
    Bird Sings
An Ideal Husband
Iliad
The Importance of Being
    Earnest
In Our Time
Inherit the Wind
Invisible Man
The Island of Dr. Moreau
Jane Eyre
Jazz
The Jew of Malta
The Joy Luck Club
Julius Caesar
Jungle of Cities
Kama Sutra
Kidnapped
King Lear
The Kite Runner
Last of the Mohicans
Leviathan
Libation Bearers
Life is Beautiful
Light In August
The Lion, the Witch and
    the Wardrobe
Lolita
Long Day's Journey Into
    Night

Lord Jim
Lord of the Flies
The Lord of the Rings:
    The Fellowship of the
    Ring
The Lord of the Rings:
    The Return of the
    King
The Lord of the Rings:
    The Two Towers
A Lost Lady
Love in the Time of
    Cholera
The Love Song of J.
    Alfred Prufrock
Lucy
Macbeth
Madame Bovary
Manhattan Transfer
Mansfield Park
MAUS
The Mayor of
    Casterbridge
Measure for Measure
Medea
Merchant of Venice
Metamorphoses
The Metamorphosis
Middlemarch
Midsummer Night's
    Dream
Moby Dick
Moll Flanders
Mother Courage and Her
    Children
Mrs. Dalloway

For our full list of over 250 Study Guides, Quizzes,
Sample College Application Essays, Literature Essays and E-texts, visit:

www.gradesaver.com

ClassicNotes

GradeSaver™

Getting you the grade since 1999™

Other ClassicNotes from GradeSaver™

Much Ado About
Nothing
My Antonia
Native Son
Night
No Exit
Notes from Underground
O Pioneers
The Odyssey
Oedipus Rex / Oedipus
the King
Of Mice and Men
The Old Man and the Sea
On Liberty
On the Road
One Day in the Life of
Ivan Denisovich
One Flew Over the
Cuckoo's Nest
One Hundred Years of
Solitude
Oroonoko
Othello
Our Town
Pale Fire
Paradise Lost
A Passage to India
The Pearl
The Picture of Dorian
Gray
Poems of W.B. Yeats:
The Rose
Portrait of the Artist as a
Young Man
Pride and Prejudice
Prometheus Bound

Pudd'nhead Wilson
Pygmalion
Rabbit, Run
A Raisin in the Sun
The Real Life of
Sebastian Knight
Red Badge of Courage
The Republic
Richard II
Richard III
The Rime of the Ancient
Mariner
Robinson Crusoe
Roll of Thunder, Hear
My Cry
Romeo and Juliet
A Room of One's Own
A Room With a View
Rosencrantz and
Guildenstern Are
Dead
Salome
The Scarlet Letter
The Scarlet Pimpernel
Secret Sharer
Sense and Sensibility
A Separate Peace
Shakespeare's Sonnets
Siddhartha
Silas Marner
Sir Gawain and the
Green Knight
Sister Carrie
Six Characters in Search
of an Author
Slaughterhouse Five

Snow Falling on Cedars
The Social Contract
Something Wicked This
Way Comes
Song of Roland
Sons and Lovers
The Sorrows of Young
Werther
The Sound and the Fury
The Spanish Tragedy
Spring Awakening
The Stranger
A Streetcar Named
Desire
The Sun Also Rises
Tale of Two Cities
The Taming of the Shrew
The Tempest
Tender is the Night
Tess of the D'Urbervilles
Their Eyes Were
Watching God
Things Fall Apart
The Threepenny Opera
The Time Machine
Titus Andronicus
To Build a Fire
To Kill a Mockingbird
To the Lighthouse
Treasure Island
Troilus and Cressida
Turn of the Screw
Twelfth Night
Ulysses
Uncle Tom's Cabin
Utopia

For our full list of over 250 Study Guides, Quizzes,
Sample College Application Essays, Literature Essays and E-texts, visit:

www.gradesaver.com

ClassicNotes

GradeSaver™

Getting you the grade since 1999™

Made in the USA
Lexington, KY
15 February 2010